PC Buyer's Handbook 2003

PC Buyer's Handbook 2003

by GORDON P. FOREMAN

McFarland & Company, Inc., Publishers
Jefferson, North Carolina, and London

ISBN 0-7864-1517-7 / ISSN 1522-838X

(softcover : 50# alkaline paper) ∞

Library of Congress cataloguing data are available

British Library cataloguing data are available

Manufactured in the United States of America

Cover image ©2003 Photospin

McFarland & Company, Inc., Publishers
Box 611, Jefferson, North Carolina 28640
www.mcfarlandpub.com

CONTENTS

INTRODUCTION

If you are thinking about buying or upgrading a computer, then you have come to the right place for help and advice. *PC Buyer's Handbook* should answer most of your questions, and give you the information that you need to make a wise computer purchase. After reading it you should know how to ask the right questions and understand the answers. Of course, once a book is printed it is quickly out of date, especially when it deals with the rapidly moving field of personal computers. To compensate, *PC Buyer's Handbook* is revised and updated each year.

E-mail comments about *PC Buyer's Handbook* (*gforeman@ix.netcom.com*) are always welcome. I want this book to cover—directly, simply, and briefly—all the common questions that people have about purchasing a new PC. Furthermore, the chapters and headings are arranged to make it easy for readers to find the sections that matter to them, without having to read a bunch of stuff that they don't care about. Furthermore, words or terms that are defined in the Glossary appear in boldface type the first time they are used in each chapter, so that you will know that you can flip to the back and look them up. I have tried to keep jargon to a minimum, but you cannot discuss computers without understanding the vocabulary, and I have worked hard to ensure that there are no common computer terms related to purchasing a computer that are not defined or explained in this book.

I have found that I tend to tell people more than they want to know, much like the parents whose first grade son sat down to dinner and asked "What is sex?" His parents choked briefly, then, having prepared for this moment, launched into an appropriate discussion of the birds and bees. The more they explained, the more frustrated he became. When they asked him what was the matter, he replied "I know that stuff, but I can't write all that in two little boxes marked 'M' and 'F'"!

Given my tendency to talk birds and bees, while the other person wants to know "M" and "F," I have tried to keep the main chapters of this book brief and to the point by moving extended explanations to the Appendix and Glossary.

Note: If you are not a regular computer user, or if you find yourself struggling to understand many of the terms used in this book, I recommend that you first read through the glossary at the end of this book, or at least refer to it frequently.

1

Where Do I Start?

There are many reasons to own a computer. You may want to work at home, or feel that your children are at a disadvantage in school if they don't have a home computer (and they are, although just like television, parental supervision is needed to avoid inappropriate material or endless hours spent on games). You may want access to the **Internet*** or to be able to stay in touch with family and friends by **e-mail**, or perhaps you want easy access to **word processor** or budget **software**. If you purchase a computer without first having a clear idea of *why* you want one, then you are likely to wind up with a system that costs more than it needs to, but that still may not meet your needs.

If you have never owned a computer, then the first question that you need to answer is whether or not to get a computer at all. A computer is a big investment, and will probably be obsolete, with essentially no resale value, within 3–4 years from the time you buy it. On the other hand, most computers sold today are bought by people who already have one or more computers, and who want a new system that will handle the demands of the latest operating system and software. For guidance in deciding what makes the most sense for your needs and budget, keep on reading!

Regardless of your primary uses, most systems sold today have enough power, but some applications, like games and multimedia, need substantially more power than word processing, or e-mail. Generally, I recommend that people get systems that are one or two notches below

Words that are defined or explained in the Glossary are placed in* **bold print *the first time they occur in each chapter.*

the fastest available, but still close to the leading edge. There are two reasons for this. First, the most recent addition to any component is the most likely to have unresolved bugs or problems, and no user really wants to deal with these problems. Second, there is usually a considerable price premium on the very latest model, and most of us have no need to pay an extra 20–50 percent to get an extra 2–5 percent of performance.

On the other hand, the power of computers has increased so rapidly that even those at the very low end of the market today are adequate for the vast majority of home uses, although as software demands continue to increase, they will become obsolete more quickly. As you read through *PC Buyer's Handbook*, you should be able to zero in on where your performance and price needs meet.

2

WHAT KIND OF SYSTEM?

There are two choices that you need to make at the very beginning, and both choices should be fairly easy. The first is: Do you want a **PC** or a **Macintosh**? The second is: Do you want a desktop system or a portable?

PC or Mac?

The PC/Mac choice should be largely determined by **compatibility** with what you are already using or want to use. If you work in a strictly PC environment, then you probably don't want to get a Mac for home, and vice versa. Of course, life is rarely so simple, so while you may have PCs at work, your children may be using Macs at school. In a case like this, I recommend that you get whichever system you can get the most help with, or that you feel the most comfortable with.

Price is not a major factor here, although a full setup of Macintosh hardware may cost a little more than an equivalent PC system. If a Mac is what you really want, then it is probably worth spending the extra 20–30 percent that an equivalent Mac **configuration** will cost.

By and large, Macs are better at running PC **software**, reading **DOS floppies**, etc., than PCs are at working with Mac software. For most users, however, a Mac will be used to run PC software only when absolutely necessary, so get the system that you will use the most. Macs have a reputation for being easier to use (the difference used to be a lot greater than it is today), but no matter which system you get, if you are a novice, you are going to need help from an experienced user for a while. Also, PCs now outsell Macs by over twelve to one, so it is more likely that you will need to know how to use a PC. Apple now appears to be profitable again, but there is little prospect that Macs will become more than a niche product any time soon.

Finally, a personal observation. If you are just getting started, and have no reason, such as compatibility with work or school, to choose one system over the other, I recommend a PC. I have noted that most PC users can switch to a Mac fairly easily, while Mac users find it much more painful to switch to a PC. Since you may run into either one, it is good to be "bilingual," and this is much easier if you first learn to use a PC. Finally, this book is intended primarily for the person who is considering the purchase of a PC, since the Mac arena offers fewer choices and less confusion. In any case, many of the issues you face as a buyer are the same for either platform.

Desktop or Portable?

Now to the second question: Should you get a desktop system (this includes tower designs as well) with **monitor**, **printer**, keyboard, etc. or a portable (i.e., a "notebook" computer)? This depends on your needs. If you spend a lot of time traveling, then you will probably want a **laptop** or **notebook** computer that can travel with you. These systems now have enough power to perform nearly all of the tasks that required a desktop system in the past, but there are still a few areas in which they simply are not as good (a smaller screen and lack of a separate numeric keypad are shortcomings for many uses.)

If you are really a candidate for a notebook computer, then you probably already have (or have owned) a desktop system, either at home or at work, although there are a few people whose needs are satisfied with only a portable system. Even if you are looking to purchase a notebook computer, I recommend that you read carefully the section on Desktop Systems before going to the chapter on Notebooks. This will give you a better background to understand what is written about Notebooks. Desktop systems are discussed in Chapter 3, while portable systems are covered in Chapter 4.

Should you build your own system?

If you are comfortable with basic electronics and can follow directions, then you can certainly build your own computer, but it will probably cost more than buying one already assembled. The reason is that computer companies buy parts wholesale for less than you can, and the labor cost to assemble a system is less than $50. Therefore, they can sell you an assembled system for less than you would pay for the various parts.

Another advantage to buying a complete system is the warranty. If you buy the parts and assemble the system yourself, and it doesn't work, then the maker of each component may blame the other component makers for the problem. If, however, you buy an assembled system, the dealer has an obligation to make the system work.

If you really want the experience of assembling your own computer, I recommend that you buy a complete system, set up your video camera, and videotape the complete process of taking it apart and putting it back together again. This can be quite educational, and if you are careful, should not cause any problems. The video camera is there in case you have trouble remembering just how things should go.

An Elaborate Pentium IV Ad.

	Discussed on pages
2.4 GHz Pentium IV CPU w/ 533 MHz system bus	9–16
Plug and Play Flash BIOS	9–16
FCC Class B approved	9–16
256 MB SDRAM upgradeable to 2 GB	16–18
80 GB 7200 rpm EIDE hard drive	18–20
750 MB internal Zip drive	18–20
3.5" 1.44 MB floppy drive	21–22
16X DVD-ROM drive	22–23
12 × 10 × 40 CD-RW drive with Roxio Easy CD Creator	22–23
SoundBlaster AWE64 PCI 3D Sound card	22–23
80 watt Stereo Speakers	22–23
MPEG 3D AGP 8X Video card with 32 MB RAM (Upgradeable to 64 MB)	23–27
19" digital NI SVGA flat-screen monitor 18.1" vis. (1600 × 1200)	23–27
56K V.90 internal voice/fax/modem	27–30
10/100 RJ45 Ethernet port	30–32
2 serial ports with 16550 UART	30–32
1 parallel port with ECP/EPP	30–32
1 Game port	30–32
1 Firewire IEEE 1394 port	30–32
4 USB ports, (2 in front USB 2.0)	30–32
Mid-tower case with 7 drive bays/200 watt power supply	32–33
104-key keyboard	34–36
Upgrade to Microsoft Ergonomic Keyboard add $59	34–36
Microsoft Optical Intelli-Mouse (PS/2)	36–37
Windows XP Home/Microsoft Works 2003 on CD	38
3-year parts/labor warranty, 1-year onsite	38–39
Toll-Free tech support for the life of the system	39–40

3

Desktop Systems *or* How to Read an Ad

Before you shop for a computer, you need to be able to read ads and understand what they mean. A typical ad for a computer looks something like the one on the previous page, although most have less detail. The number to the right of each line or lines indicates the section in this chapter where that topic is discussed. The relevant lines also appear under the heading for each section.

CPU, BIOS, Chipset, etc.

2.4 GHz Pentium IV CPU w/ 533 MHz system bus

Plug and Play Flash BIOS

FCC Class B approved

CPU stands for Central Processing Unit and is the chip that is the actual "brain" of the computer. The major CPUs used in PCs today are **Celerons** or **Pentium IVs** from Intel, and the **Athlon** and **Duron** family from AMD. There are many **486** and Pentium class computers still in use, but nearly all systems sold today have one of the above chips in them.

Intel has stopped manufacturing Pentium through Pentium III CPUs for desktop systems in favor of the Pentium IV, and even the

Celeron line of CPUs, which is their low end, now includes the added instruction sets that distinguish the **P4** (the Pentium IV is often referred to this way) from earlier versions. The chief distinctions between the Pentium IV and the Celeron are in the **cache** size and the system bus design. The Pentium IV has an internal cache of 32 KB and an external cache of 512 KB, while the Celeron has the same 32 KB internal cache, but an external cache of only 128 KB. The front system bus refers to how fast the CPU can communicate with the memory or RAM of the system. The PIV CPUs can typically communicate at up to 533 MHz, while the Celeron is limited to 400 MHz. These differences don't affect performance as much as you might guess. If you compare benchmarks for a Celeron and a P4, both running at the same clock speed on otherwise identical systems, the P4 will be slightly faster (in the range of 5–25 percent) for most benchmarks. Of course, the fastest P4 CPUs are significantly faster than the fastest Celeron CPUs (3.0 GHz vs. 2.0 GHz as of November 2002), so if you are looking for a system on the high end, you probably do not want a Celeron.

Intel's flagship CPU, the **Pentium IV**, has been available since early 2001, although its speed and other refinements have improved performance extensively since its introduction. It started out at 1.4 GHz, and by November 2002 had reached 3.0 GHz, with faster speeds promised.

In the summer of 1999, AMD introduced the **Athlon** CPU, running at 500 or 600 MHz, with speeds as I write this as high as 2.0 GHz, although it will likely be faster by the time you read this. Actually, AMD refers to the current line of Athlon CPUs as the XP series, and assigns them a number that supposedly correlates to the equivalent Pentium. For example, an Athlon XP2000 is advertised as being roughly equivalent to a 2.0 GHz Pentium IV, although it actually runs at 1.67 GHz. The reason for the difference is that the Athlon CPUs process data more efficiently than the P4, although the differences are very much a function of what type of data is being processed. The AMD Athlon shines on business related tasks, although even at best it is only slightly better than an equivalent P4, while the P4 is substantially faster on tasks such as creating multimedia, video editing, etc. However, for most common desktop computing tasks, the differences in performance between the top of the line Intel and AMD CPUs is so small that users will not be aware of the difference from day to day. No doubt many people will stick with Intel CPUs simply because they are more common, and many leading companies appear reluctant to offend Intel by trading with AMD, but companies such as Hewlett Packard, IBM, and Compaq, as well as a host of lesser names, now offer systems with Athlon CPUs. I personally own a homebuilt system with an Athlon 1.3 GHz CPU, and I have not had any problems with it that appear to be in any way associated with the CPU.

At the low end of the market, most systems use either the Celeron CPU from Intel, or the Duron CPU from AMD. Complete systems, including 1.7 GHz CPU, 128 MB RAM, a 20–30 GB hard drive, CD-ROM drive, sound card, 56 kbps modem, 15" monitor, etc., are available for under $500, or even under $400 without a Windows operating system. However, since most people will want to go ahead and get the latest technology, especially as it costs only a few hundred dollars more, the discussion that follows will focus primarily on the Pentium IV and/or Athlon systems.

Also, you should be aware that even though they look virtually identical, motherboards must be designed for either the AMD or Intel CPUs. They are not interchangeable! The Intel CPUs use a 478-pin socket, while the AMD CPUs use a 462-pin socket (usually referred to as Socket A). This is the big white square on the picture of the motherboard.

The **ATX** motherboards that all modern systems use incorporate a design that makes it easier to get to the CPU and SIMM sockets, while also reducing the problem of SIMMs or CPUs that block long **cards** in some of the **slots**. The ATX power supply also allows the operating system to shut down the computer, or to start it up from a remote signal, such as a telephone call to a modem or a signal over a network.

There are currently a variety of chipsets in use, and they tend to change very quickly. As a prospective computer buyer, rather than focusing on a particular **chipset**, you should make sure that whatever you get supports at least the following: 133 MHz PCI support (also known as **BSB** or backside bus), 266 MHz **SDRAM** (also known as **FSB** or front side bus), 133 MHz IDE connection to hard drives, and **AGP 4x** video. Although it may support **RDRAM**, it should also support the more common (and much less expensive) SDRAM and **DDR** RAM. Most Pentium IV systems built through the third quarter of 2001 could only use RDRAM, but thanks to new chipsets from Intel and Via, most new Pentium systems can now use SDRAM as well. (See the sections on Cache, RAM, and Ports that follow for more explanation of these features.)

This is a motherboard from a computer that uses an Athlon CPU. The design drawing on the facing page is for the same motherboard, and identifies the major parts.

Computers can generate interference with radio and TV, so to control this, the FCC (Federal Communications Commission) requires that systems be tested to verify that such emissions are kept below levels that will normally interfere. Class B certification is appropriate for home use, and is more stringent than Class A, which is targeted to business office use (where presumably, not a lot of people are watching TV all day). In addition to radio and TV interference, if you notice that your monitor seems distorted, try moving your speakers away from the sides of the monitor. The speakers generate a magnetic field, which can interfere with the electron beams that generate the image on the computer screen. This is not a problem with a flat-panel monitor.

A **heat sink** is a small radiator that keeps CPUs cool enough to

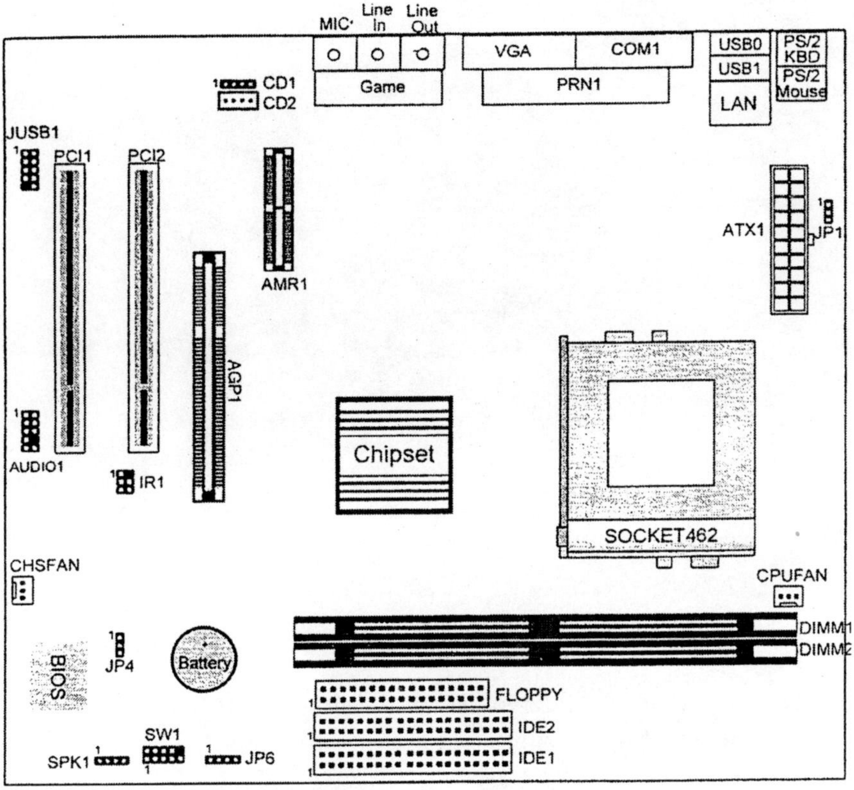

keep them from melting down a system or burning out. Virtually all Pentium and Athlon systems come with a cooling module that extends over an inch above the CPU with a fan on top of that, in order to keep the temperature of the CPU within a safe operating range.

Some systems come with a Peltier heat sink, which is a solid-state cooling unit that actually refrigerates the CPU to help keep it cool. These cost a few dollars more, and add a 50–80 watt load to your power supply, so use them cautiously. Also, be aware that while they cool the CPU they add a lot more heat to the interior of your computer, so you need to have very good fans and circulation inside the box if a Peltier is installed.

The **BIOS** or Basic Input/Output System is the chip that controls basic **I/O** functions. Until the last few years, the BIOS was on a chip where it could not be modified short of removing and replacing it, but now most companies are shipping systems with a **flash** BIOS (i.e., a BIOS that can be reprogrammed). The manufacturer can then send you

This is a heatsink for an Athlon CPU with a cooling fan attached to the top.

a floppy disk with an updated BIOS, or you can **download** one by **modem**. There are also companies that sell upgrade BIOS chips for older systems.

Plug and Play, or **PnP**, is a joint effort among Microsoft, Intel, and several other companies to develop PCs and supporting cards that can be upgraded without pain or frustration. With a PnP system, if you want to add multimedia or a **SCSI** card, or anything else, you simply turn the PC off, open the **case**, plug the **card** into an open **slot**, and turn the computer back on. The computer recognizes the new card, prompts you to insert the driver disk that (hopefully) came with it, and **configures** itself so that everything works together. You no longer have to fiddle with IRQs*, DMA channels, base memory addresses, **jumpers**, **DIP switches**, etc. Virtually all systems now on the market support PnP, although it doesn't always work as easily as advertised. And, of course, you need to save the floppy disks or CDs that come with the drivers for each component of your system, in case you ever need to reinstall them. If you cannot provide the proper drivers,

You don't really want explanations for each of these, do you? If you do, see the list of references in the Appendix. Most of the general PC hardware books explain them thoroughly.

then items such as video cards, sound cards, etc., will not work properly or have access to all of their features. Of course, if you know the name of the company that produced the item, then you can almost always find drivers on the Internet. Microsoft has also included drivers for many common cards in the operating system itself, so that you need do nothing other than reboot the system a time or two. The more up-to-date the operating system, the more drivers that are typically installed.

The PnP hardware specification requires a PnP-compliant **operating system** or **OS. Windows 98, Windows ME, Windows 2000** and **Windows XP** are all PNP operating systems.

The **motherboard** is the board in the bottom of the case that holds the CPU, **RAM**, etc., along with the **slots** into which **cards** are installed. The photo and drawing that you saw on the previous pages are of an Athlon motherboard. There are four types of **bus** (slots) that are in wide use on PCs. The oldest of these is the **ISA** bus, which is a 16-**bit** bus (that is, it will pass data 16 bits at a time) that runs at 8 MHz. The ISA bus originated with the PC AT back in 1984, and is very antiquated, but is available on very few systems today. Most of the capabilities that relied on the ISA bus in the past have been moved to PCI, incorporated into the motherboard, or are provided through a USB connection.

Many systems, especially at the lower end of the price range, now ship with motherboards that have built in to them all the common functions that used to be provided by add-on cards, and still are in the higher-end systems. These include sound, video, and **10/100 network,** in addition to the serial, parallel, USB, keyboard and mouse ports that are part of nearly all current motherboards. The tradeoff is that while the cost is less, you are not getting high-end components. At the same time, unless you are into serious game playing or other demanding applications, these systems are good enough for nearly all uses, and if you decide to upgrade to a better video or sound card, you can disable the ones on the motherboard and install new ones that meet all your wants.

PCI local bus is a 32-bit bus that runs at 33 MHz, 66 MHz, or even 133 MHz on newer motherboards. Thus, a PCI card can communicate with the CPU much faster than an ISA card. The PCI bus was introduced by Intel shortly after the introduction of the Pentium CPU, and is about ten years newer than the ISA bus, although the PCI standard has been enhanced extensively since that time. The primary uses for PCI slots are video cards, hard drive **controllers, SCSI**

controllers, and network cards, since these benefit most from higher speeds. PCI modems and sound cards are now quite common as well, primarily because they are easier to configure, since PCI peripherals are designed to be inherently compatible with PnP. There are two PCI slots on the motherboard in the picture.

The third type of port is the Accelerated Graphics Port, or **AGP**, which Intel introduced in early 1998. It is used only for AGP video controllers, and provides much faster video updates without adding to the load on the PCI bus.

Finally, there is the **AMR** or audio modem riser slot, which allows a modem to be added to a system while minimizing the interference that is common between the modem's analog interface and the fully digital circuitry of the motherboard.

Cache

Cache comes in two flavors, although thanks to advances in chip design, they now taste about the same. First there is the internal (L1) 32**K** cache that comes standard on Pentium and Athlon CPUs. This is called internal because it has been built into the CPU itself since the 486 model, and runs at the same speed as the CPU. Then there is the external (or **L2**) cache that used to sit on the motherboard next to the CPU, but that is now built right into the CPU just like the L1 cache. The size of the L2 cache can range anywhere from 128K on Celeron CPUs to 512K on the P4. The reason for maintaining two kinds of cache appears to be a consequence of the basic CPU design, which can only access 32K of L1 cache, but functionally, there is now little difference between the L1 and L2 caches.

(For more information on how cache works, see the Appendix.)

A third kind of cache is software cache, but that is covered under hard drives.

RAM

256 MB DDR SDRAM upgradeable to 2 GB

RAM (random access memory) is the system memory. It holds the data and programs that the computer is working with. 128 **MB** (mega-

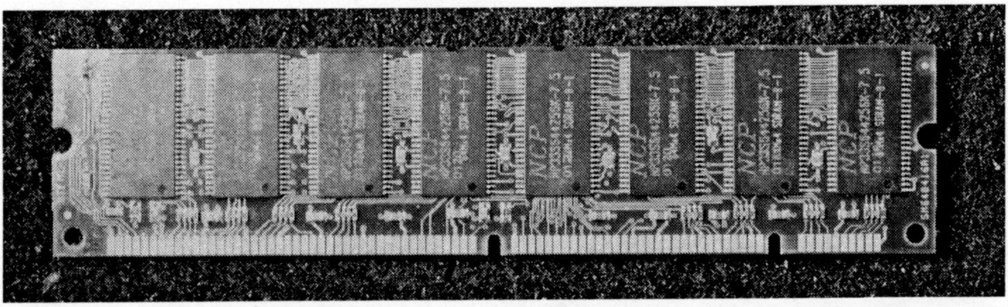

This is a picture of an SDRAM DIMM, typical of those used in many systems. This one has a capacity of 512 MB.

bytes) is the minimum you should consider on a new system, and unless you are on a really tight budget, I recommend 512 MB or more. Now that RAM prices have dropped so much, most systems are shipping with 128 MB or more. Of course, it's usually not hard to add RAM later on, so if you start with less, it's not a disaster. (Q: Hard disks and RAM are both measured in MB. What is the difference between them? A: See the Appendix for an explanation of the differences.)

Most system RAM in Pentium IV systems comes in the form of **SDRAM**, or Synchronous Dynamic Random Access Memory (pronounced s-d-ram), although **RDRAM** or Rambus DRAM is implemented in all P4 systems built before September 2001. However, RDRAM is much more expensive than SDRAM, so Intel developed a new chipset that supports both kinds, in order to be more competitive with AMD, which has always used the SDRAM. Synchronous means that the speed and clock cycle of the RAM is controlled by the CPU, so as to minimize the time lost when either accessing or storing data. SDRAM modules are also called **DIMMs**, or Dual In-line Memory Modules, which refers to the actual physical format of the RAM. They may also be called 168-pin DIMMs, which refers to the number of electrical contacts through which signals are transmitted.

Another innovation that is often used is **DDR** or double data rate RAM. This consists of standard SDRAM, which means that it is relatively inexpensive. The double data rate comes into play by reading data from different locations in RAM on alternating cycles of the CPU, and thus managing to read (in theory) twice as much data from memory as would otherwise be possible. DDR RAM is only possible where the system BIOS supports it, although it is incorporated into a number of video cards as well.

If a system suffers spontaneous glitches, including sudden reboots without warning, lockups of various different programs or the system as a whole, without any consistent pattern, then a bad RAM module is a likely source of the problem. If the problem is consistent, meaning that every time you do a particular action, things crash, then RAM is not likely the cause of the problem, but with random problems, be suspicious of the RAM.

Hard Drive/Removable Drive

80 GB 7200 rpm EIDE hard drive

750 MB Internal ZIP drive

Over the last several years, **hard drive** prices have dropped by nearly 50 percent per year when calculated in cost per MB (see Figure A-3 in the Appendix). A dozen years ago a 120 MB hard drive was large for a home system, and 80 MB was more common. Now, the minimum hard drive you should get for a home system is 40 **GB** or 40,000 MB, and drives up to nearly 160 GB and larger are now available, with even larger ones coming soon. **Disk compression** can also increase storage, but for more on that, see the Appendix.

The 7200 rpm refers to how fast the drive platters spin. Until a couple of years ago, the standard speed was 5400 rpm, and while these drives are still available, the faster ones cost very little more, and are preferred. Drives running at 7200 rpm will typically have an **average seek time** of 9 milliseconds or less, which means that it takes it, on average, 9 thousandths of a second to locate a non-sequential bit of information. Of course, most programs consist of thousands or millions of bits, so even with a fast hard drive (and 9 **ms** is fairly fast) it may take several seconds to load a program. A dozen years ago hard drives had seek times of 65–80 ms, and eight years ago 28–40 ms was common. The fastest hard drives today have seek times around 6 ms, and the slowest are around 12 ms.

Even though 9 ms sounds fast, it is nearly a million times slower than data access from RAM, so hard drives manufacturers now add a 64K or larger hardware **cache** that holds the data on the disk that appears sequentially after what was just asked for. Then, if that is the data needed

The hard drive on the left is a 30 MB drive that was built in 1987. The one on the right is a laptop hard drive 2.5 inches wide that holds 30 GB, or 1000 times as much. The drive in the middle is a standard 3.5-inch hard drive that holds 40 GB, although much higher capacities are available.

next, as it often is, it is available in billionths of a second rather than thousandths of a second, greatly speeding data access.

New hard drives are usually **Enhanced IDE** (or **EIDE**) drives. They are sometimes designated as **ATA** drives, but these are just two different names for the same thing. Two EIDE **controllers** are built in to all motherboards now, each of which supports two drives, allowing the system to have up to four EIDE drives, which can be hard drives, Zip drives, CD-ROM drives, DVD-ROM drives, or CD-RW drives.

High end computers or workstations, especially those designed for **CAD** or engineering, often come with **SCSI** (pronounced scuzzy) drives, rather than IDE. A single SCSI controller can support up to seven devices (or even fifteen devices with ultra-wide SCSI) and those devices can include **scanners**, tape backups, **Jaz** drives, CD-RW drives, etc., in addition to hard drives and CD-ROM drives. Furthermore, a modern SCSI controller handles data faster than IDE, so for high-end applications, SCSI is a better choice. However, it also costs more, which is why it is not included as standard equipment on most systems. For most home and office applications, IDE is good enough. Of course, EIDE and SCSI drives and **peripherals** can work together with no problems, so there is no reason to insist on one or the other; you can have both.

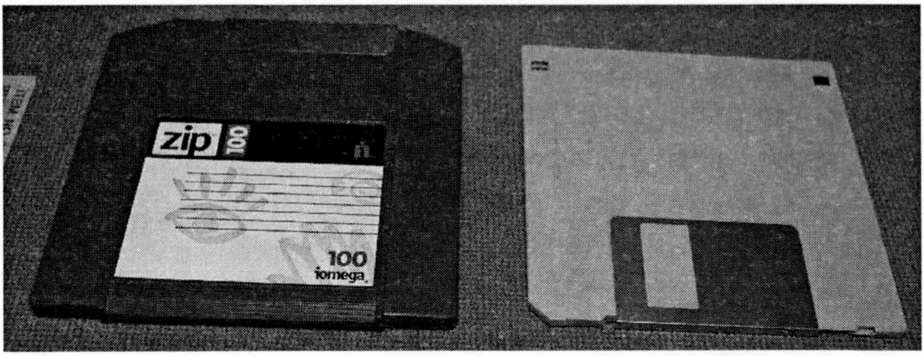

This is a picture of a 100 MB Zip disk (the 250 MB disks are exactly the same size and shape) next to a 1.44 MB floppy disk. The sizes are similar, but the Zip holds much more.

The Iomega **Zip drive**, which holds 750 MB, is now available as either an internal or an external drive. (External means that it is not mounted inside the computer case like the floppy drive, but sits in its own case near or on the computer.) Older Zip drives that only hold 100 MB or 250 MB per disk are very common. The 750 MB drives have no problem reading and writing to 250 MB disks, and will read but not write to the 100 MB disks, but on a new system I would expect to get a 750 MB Zip drive. Many systems now come with a Zip drive as standard equipment, and the Zip drive is well positioned to become a replacement for the 3.5" floppy drive. The chief drawback is that it is not compatible with the 3.5" floppy, but its market share is so large, compared to its competitors, that it may not matter. The time has not yet come to drop the 3.5" floppy, but getting an internal Zip drive in a new system is definitely a good idea.

Or, if you want to be able to share one Zip drive among multiple systems, you can get an external one with a USB connection that can simply be plugged into whichever system you want, without any need to shut down or reboot the computer. This is also a good way to go if you are considering adding a Zip drive to an existing computer.

A number of other **backup** options are available, including **CDR** (recordable CD-ROM drives/disks), **CD-RW** (read/write) and tape backups. Tape backups have storage capacities up to 20 GB or more and prices that range from $200 on up. CD-RW can store only 650–700 MB per disk, depending on which disks you buy, but prices for CD-RW drives are now under $60 in many cases, and the cost of blank disks is under $0.50 each, which makes them almost throwaway items. A big advantage to CD-RW is that virtually everyone has a CD-ROM drive that will let them read the disks written on a CD-RW. However, the Zip drives read and write as much as 60 times faster and can be reused many times, while a CD-R disk can be written to only once. CD-RW is typically slower than CD-R, but can be written to and erased multiple times. It should be noted here that CD-RW drives can also write to CD-R disks, although it still requires a special program, such as Roxio's Easy CD Creator for **burning CDs**.

The numbers that follow the drive (12 × 10 × 40) refer to how fast the drive performs each category of reading or writing. Writing to CD-R disks it runs at 12×, or 12 times the speed of an audio CD. Writing to a CD-RW, it runs at 10×, and reading data, at 40×.

There are also several kinds of **DVD** recorders on the market now as well, although they cost somewhat more than CD-RW, but the real drawback is that they are not always compatible among themselves. That is, disks recorded on one kind of drive may not be readable on a different type. Of course, if you are primarily interested in backing up data for your own system, then that may not be such a problem, and they do have capacities in excess of 4 GB per disk.

Tape backups are much slower than any of the other options mentioned here, but are widely used because they have capacities of 10–20 GB or more. For nearly all users, a removable drive of some sort is recommended over tape backups, although this is not true for backup of network servers or large drive arrays.

Note: All users should have (and use!) some sort of backup. There are only two kinds of computer users, those who have lost data, and those who will lose data. If you don't want to be both kinds, back up your data frequently. It is relatively easy to reinstall applications, but files that you have created or modified yourself can be gone forever if your hard drive crashes, or a virus corrupts your file system, or even if your kids delete files that they shouldn't.

Floppy Drives

3.5" 1.44 MB floppy drive

A 3.5" **floppy drive** is still an essential item for most computer users, but that may not be true in another year or two. At some point, there will be a move away from the 3.5" floppy to some other sort of disk with higher capacity. The Zip drive appears to be the leading candidate for now, but it is still too soon to contemplate leaving a 3.5" floppy off of a new system.

CD-ROM Drives/Multimedia

10× DVD-ROM drive

12 × 10 × 40 CD-RW drive

SoundBlaster AWE64 PCI 3D Sound card

80 watt Stereo Speakers

Until 1993, **CD-ROM** drives were a special-use accessory, but they are now being superseded by either CD-RW or DVD-ROM, both of which can still read CDs just fine, but which add other capabilities. (See Figure A-5 in the Appendix.)

Although you can still buy very low-end systems with just a CD-ROM drive, most systems sold now include a **CD-RW** or rewritable CD-ROM drive. These drives allow you to read existing CDs, but also let you make your own CD-ROM disks from data on your system. Even if you decide to get a CD-RW, it is usually a good idea to have a **DVD-ROM** drive installed too. Not only does this provide additional performance, it also facilitates the process of copying CDs. While I strongly encourage people to abide by copyright laws, there are times when the ability to back up a CD can be invaluable.

The next generation of capacity beyond the CD-ROM is the DVD-ROM or digital video disk, with storage capacities seven to twenty-eight times greater than a CD-ROM, but on the same size disk. This is sufficient to record a full two-hour movie on one disk, so their entertainment potential is as larger or larger than the purely computer applications. Prices are still about forty dollars higher than for plain CD-ROM drives, but DVD-ROM is moving rapidly into the mainstream, especially on home systems. Business systems are still configured in many cases with CD-ROM or CD-RW drives, primarily because the entertainment demand is not there, but since DVD-ROM device drivers are included Windows 2000 and XP, business systems are also migrating to DVD-ROM drives, and before much longer, it is likely that the simple CD-ROM will cease to be available on new systems.

DVD recording drives are now available, at a cost of $250 and higher, but there are so many different formats (including DVD+RW, DVD-R, DVD+R, DVD-RW, and DVD-RAM), mostly incompatible with each other, that I only recommend a DVD burner for a home system if you are using it for backing up your hard drive, or if you know exactly what you will use it for, and are sure you can get the right format.

CD-ROMs are closely associated with **multimedia** kits, which means adding a sound card and speakers to the system. Sound capabilities are essential if you plan to play games on your system, or if you intend for your children to use it for educational purposes. Virtually all systems today come with sound cards installed, or built into the motherboard, even those designed for an office environment, so whether or not to get sound is not usually a consideration, and most modern sound cards are adequate for whatever uses you may have in mind, although **voice recognition** software may not work well if your sound card is not adequate.

Speakers may be more of a concern. Most new systems will come with speakers that are adequate for games, but if you want to listen to music CDs, or experience the full effects of 3D sound, you may need to upgrade to a better speaker set. In particular, high-end sound cards now come with two speaker ports, allowing you to install two sets of speakers, one in front on each side of the monitor, and another set behind you such that you can be immersed in a 3D sound environment. This can add a powerful new dimension to games, as sound can now provide much more precise clues as to what is going on outside of the player's field of view.

Monitors and Video Cards

MPEG 3D AGP 8× Video card with 32 MB RAM (upgradeable to 64 MB)

19" digital NI SVGA flat-screen monitor 18.1" vis. (1600 × 1200)

Virtually all **monitors** sold today are capable of **VGA** and **SVGA** resolution. VGA is 640 **pixels** wide by 480 pixels high (pixel is short

This shows a keyboard tray that fits under a monitor stand, and which allows a comfortable work area on a table that is otherwise too narrow for both a monitor and a keyboard.

for picture element, and is one dot on the screen). SVGA can be 800 × 600, 1024 × 768 or higher. VGA is the standard resolution that all monitors can display, but most people prefer to run at a higher resolution if they can.

15" monitors come only with very low-end systems, and while they may be capable of displaying SVGA resolutions, the resulting characters and images are so small that most people will not bother with resolutions above 800 × 600. I recommend that you get at least a 17" monitor, which is quite comfortable at 1024 × 768, or if you have space for it, a 19" monitor, which is quite good at 1280 × 1024, although many users also like 1024 × 768 on a 19" monitor. A 17" monitor may cost as little as $120, while 19" monitors start about $80–$100 higher.

Another dimension to pay close attention to is the depth of the monitor from front to back. A typical 17" monitor will be at least 17" from front to back, and this does not include the 1–2" needed for the video and power cables. Since many people plan to use a desk that is no more than 24" from front to back, a 17" monitor may not leave room in front for a keyboard, unless a keyboard tray or extender of some sort is added. And speaking of a keyboard tray, most people will need some way to support the monitor at least 2–4" above the desktop, in order to have an ergonomically balanced relationship between the height of the keyboard, monitor, and eyes of the user. A keyboard tray is an excellent way to take care of all these needs at once.

Note: Although monitors are advertised as 15", 17", etc., you should be aware that the size refers to the size of the cathode ray tube (**CRT**), and not the viewable screen area. In general, a 15" monitor will actually measure slightly less than 14" from corner to corner, while a 17" monitor will measure around 16" and a 19" monitor around 18". In this ad, the 18.1" vis means that this monitor has 18.1" of visible screen, corner to corner.

Although computers are typically sold with monitors, you should consider the monitor to be a separate item. The reason is that monitors do not become outdated as fast as computers do, and while you may want or need to upgrade a computer after two to three years, a monitor may serve you well for twice that long or more. If your monitor is still adequate for your needs, then you can save $150–$350 or more by buying a new computer without a monitor. Of course, if you buy a computer with the monitor built into the unit, like the iMac or some low-end PC models, then these considerations are irrelevant.

Another common number applied to monitors is **dot pitch**, which refers to the size of each pixel on the screen. The dot pitch is measured in millimeters, and the smaller the dot pitch the crisper the image. Dot pitches of 0.39, 0.42, and even 0.51 mm used to be common. These resulted in a fuzzy display, since each pixel on the screen would overlap with its neighbors. You should consider the maximum acceptable dot pitch to be 0.31 mm, while dot pitches of 0.28 and 0.26 mm are even better.

You may also see the word "**non-interlaced**" or NI. Nearly all monitors today are non-interlaced, which is good. Do not get an interlaced monitor. Note: Non-interlaced monitors can still run in interlaced mode. If your screen appears to flicker, or if horizontal lines appear to wiggle, check the screen **refresh** settings, and select a number of 70 Hz or higher.

Graphics adapters (video cards) control the image on the monitor. Older systems may come with a PCI graphics card, but most new systems will use AGP (Advanced Graphics Port). This is a new port developed by Intel to speed up the video input and output without bogging down the PCI bus. New AGP video cards may come with anywhere from 4 to 64 MB RAM, but the better ones have a minimum of 32 MB RAM, and many now have 64 MB. The 8× on AGP simply indicates that it is supposed to be faster than AGP, AGP 2×, or AGP 4×, which were its earlier standards.

On a 2D video card (anything more than five years old or so) the card can only track the position of each pixel on an x–y coordinate grid. The addition of 3D to video cards means that each point may also be assigned a "z" coordinate so that in 3D games and applications, closer objects will block out farther ones. This requires more RAM, so any 3D video card you get in a new system should have at least 16 MB, and if you are planning to use a 17" or larger monitor for games, get 32 MB or more.

You should also note that it is possible to have both an AGP and a PCI video card in a system together. In particular, many high-end game systems incorporate two video cards in order to obtain the smoothest and fastest 3D scrolling and panning. With Windows 98, Windows ME, Windows 2000, and Windows XP you can even have two monitors installed at once, so as to have a larger field of view or to keep two different program screens visible at the same time.

MPEG (pronounced M-peg) means that the video card supports video compression processes that will allow full-screen motion video. Thus, video clips on CD-ROMs or DVDs will play back with realistic speed and little if any jerkiness.

Virtually all monitors sold today are **flat-screen**, meaning that they don't bulge a lot in the middle as did the early monitors, but since

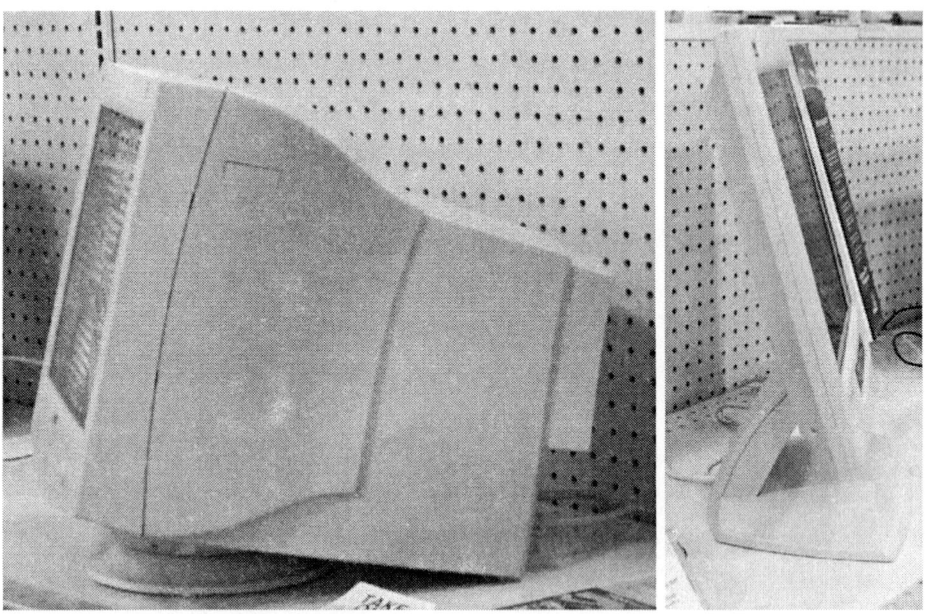

This shows the depth required for a CRT monitor, versus the small amount of room needed by a flat-panel monitor. If you are cramped for space, the flat-panel may be worth the extra money.

nearly all monitors incorporate this feature, it is not a selling point for any particular brand.

True flat-panel displays, based on the technology used in portable computers, are now widely available, although they still cost more than regular monitors. Currently a true 15" flat-panel display can be purchased for as little as $250, while 17" ones start at around $400. 19" and larger flat-panel monitors are still going to set you back at least $600, and prices range widely up from there. However, prices will continue to decline, and someday the computer monitor as we know it will be gone. Flat-panel displays have a number of advantages over CRTs. First of all, they free up large amounts of desk space by sitting near the back of the desk. Second, they are much more energy efficient, reducing electric bills and cutting down on excess heat. Third, they emit zero electromagnetic radiation, which may or may not have any effect on the health of users. Fourth, they have no flicker to them, making them easier on our eyes. Finally, they are purely digital, meaning that the processing necessary for the computer to run them is greatly reduced. Monitors now in use are analog devices, meaning that the digital signal that the computer produces has to be converted to an analog signal for the monitor. With a flat-panel display this step is eliminated, although it may require that you add a specific video card to your computer. Most flat-panel displays can convert an analog video signal, but the image is not as clear, and the overhead of converting the signal from digital to analog in the computer, and then from analog back to digital in the display slows the system down noticeably.

Fax/Modem

56K V.90 internal voice/fax/modem

A modem is the device that allows you to dial up **online services** and **log on** to the **Internet** through an **ISP** (Internet Service Provider). It sends and receives data over a phone line, which is much slower than most other kinds of data transfer, but can still be quite useful. Your first decision here is whether or not you need a modem. Your computer will run fine without one, but for most people, a primary reason for buying a computer is to connect to the Internet, and a modem typically adds only $10–$25 to the cost of a system.

Before you buy an analog modem, check whether you have access to faster options in your area. The two major choices are a **cable modem** and a **DSL** phone line. Cable modems plug into your cable TV line and provide a connection that can be up to 100 times faster than a regular modem. A potential drawback is that the cable connection is shared with all other cable modem users on your "leg" of the cable, which can slow down service when multiple users are surfing at the same time. However, the **bandwidth** is still sufficient that even with 10–20 other users, you will still see a lot better performance than with a regular modem.

A DSL (Digital Subscriber Line) phone line looks like a regular phone line, but provides a digital connection, rather than the typical analog phone signal. The speed of a DSL can vary, with faster connections costing more than slow ones, but even a slow DSL connection running at 768 kbps is over 15 times faster than an analog modem. While a DSL is nominally slower than a cable modem, it is a dedicated line, meaning that all the bandwidth is yours; you are not sharing it with other users as you are with a cable modem (unless you have multiple computers in your home that share a single DSL). Another benefit to a DSL is that it can carry multiple signals, so that you can have a phone conversation and an internet connection going all at the same time. However, DSL lines are limited to about 3.5 miles in length, meaning that if you are farther than that from your phone switching station, you can't get DSL service, even if it is nominally available in your area. If you are not sure, call your phone company, and they should be able to tell you whether or not DSL is available on your line.

Both cable modems and DSL connections are continuous connections, meaning that the network is always there in the background, with no need to dial up to create a connection. This means that you never get "logged off" if you don't display any activity for a set period of time, and when you want to surf, the network is there. I have been using a DSL connection for two years now, and I am very happy with it. Surfing the Internet is now much faster, and it feels more like the network connection that I have at work. Costs are typically on the order of $50 per month, but this includes an Internet Service Provider (**ISP**), and thus is not a lot more than the cost of an extra phone line and ISP when purchased separately.

Assuming that you don't have access to either a cable modem or DSL, I recommend that you get a **56K** modem. A **V.92** modem is one that complies with the current standard for 56K modems. For over a year there were two competing 56K standards, but V.90 merged the other two standards and eliminated the conflicts, while V.92 now includes other advances.

Most modems now have the ability to set up your computer as a voice mail system. However, very few people ever use this option. Answering machines are cheap and easy to set up, and voice-mail service through local phone companies is inexpensive and very reliable. I once set up a voice-mail system on a computer, and while it usually worked, glitches were common enough that I never had much confidence in it.

The other choice you face is whether to get an internal or external modem. External modems sit outside the case and connect to a **serial** or **USB** port, while internal modems fit in a PCI slot on the motherboard and usually configure themselves as COM3 or COM4 so that they don't interfere with one of your serial ports (COM1 or COM2). The external modem is easier to move around, and you can see lights on the front that indicate such things as dial tone, data transfer, power, etc. However, internal modems cost less, are out of the way inside your computer, and don't add to the cable clutter that grows behind nearly all computers.

Nearly all modems sold today can send and receive faxes. However, to send a fax, the document must be a file in the computer; a paper copy cannot be sent unless your system includes a **scanner**. Also, when you receive a fax, it will be stored on disk as a file, rather than being printed out. Of course, if you receive a lot of junk faxes, then this can be an excellent way of weeding through them.

Regardless of which fax/modem you get, if you expect to spend more than an hour per day using your modem, you should consider getting a second phone line installed. Call waiting must be disabled in order to **log on** to most on-line services (otherwise, incoming calls will interrupt your session), and it can be very frustrating to people trying to call you if they cannot get through for hours at a time.

Another option for high-speed Internet service is a satellite connection. These connections are available anywhere in the United States that has an unobstructed view of the southern sky, and no phone line is needed. Speeds are not generally as high as with a DSL or cable modem, but are still much faster than with a regular modem. It will probably cost around $500 to get started, with monthly bills of $70 or so, although if internet service is combined with digital satellite TV service you may be able to get discounts for package deals.

ISDN is a digital phone line technology that was first available ten years or more ago, but that has never become widely available in the United States. Other options are becoming available that are much faster, and thus more desirable.

Note: Free Internet service is offered by a number of companies, but the catch is that you have to use their software, and watch a lot of ads. If you don't mind this, then such offers may be tempting, but for most of us, the annoyance of the ads is not worth the cost savings.

Ports

2 serial ports with 16550 UART

1 parallel port with ECP/EPP, 1 Game port

1 Firewire 1394 port

4 USB 2.0 ports

10/100 RJ45 Ethernet port

Nearly all systems today come with one or two **serial** ports and a **parallel** port built into the motherboard. The serial ports are most commonly used for a **mouse** and a modem, but there are other peripherals that can plug into them. Most new systems now use a PS/2 mouse port, leaving the serial ports free, since an internal modem will usually be configured as a third serial port. The game **port** is part of the sound card.

The parallel port is used almost exclusively to connect to a printer,

Typical ports found on the back of a computer.

although such things as external Zip drives may also connect to the parallel port. ECP/EPP refers to the latest standard for parallel ports which are faster and allow the printer or other peripheral to communicate more efficiently with the computer.

Most systems now come with two, four, or six **USB** (Universal Serial Bus) ports. Although some new systems are still shipping with USB 1.1 ports, most should now come with at least 2 USB 2.0 ports. The difference is that USB 1.1 can handle data transfer speeds up to 12 Mbs (12 million bits per second), while USB 2.0 can theoretically handle speeds up to 480 Mbs. I say theoretically because there are very few devices that can either supply or receive data at that pace. USB 2.0 is fully backward compatible with 1.1, meaning that all 1.1 devices can work just fine on a 2.0 port, but there are getting to be more and more CD-RW drives, Zip drives, external hard drives, scanners, etc., that support the faster speed, and need it to transfer data more quickly, so any new system should have at least two USB 2.0 ports, and at least four USB ports total. If you need more ports, and many of us do, then USB hubs can be added externally to give up to a dozen ports or more. Theoretically, a single USB port can support up to 126 devices linked together through one port, but in practice, more than half a dozen or so USB devices per port are likely to overload a system.

One thing that makes USB peripherals so popular is that you can plug in a USB device and have the system recognize it and use it without having to reboot the system. Of course, you must have a driver installed for the device, so the first time you plug a USB peripheral in, the computer may ask for a driver disk before recognizing it. When buying a new system, I would recommend that you give preference to one that uses USB for as many peripherals as possible. Windows 98 and Windows ME both include support for USB, as do Windows 2000 and XP. As USB becomes the interface of choice for these items, and four or more USB ports become standard, it is likely that the older serial, parallel, keyboard, and mouse ports will be eliminated from new computers, but how soon this will happen is hard to say.

Firewire is the trade name attached to the IEEE standard 1394. It is a port that handles much higher speeds than USB 1.1 (but very similar to USB 2.0), up to 400 Mbps, making it suitable for such things as external hard drives, monitors, live video cameras, etc. Many systems now come with both Firewire and USB 2.0, and many of the drives and such that make use of the higher speeds can plug into either one.

This unit provides a network connection to other computers in the same home, without needing to run any wires between the systems.

Although many home users don't yet have a home network installed, the 10/100 Ethernet port is also necessary as a connection for most cable modems or DSL connections, although some networking hardware uses a USB interface. The 10/100 refers to the speed at which it operates, either 10 megabits per second, or 100 mb/sec. If it is connected to a network running at 100 mb/sec, then it will run at that speed, but given that most home networking hardware, including the Internet options mentioned above, run at less than 10 mb/sec, it will default to the slower speed. For more on setting up a home network, see the section on networks at the end of Chapter 5.

Case

Mid-tower case with 7 drive bays/200 watt ATX power supply

Computers come in a variety of cases, the major styles being the standard desktop, the mid **tower**, and the full tower. You may also find a mini case (also called a slimline) or a mini-tower, but I recommend avoiding such systems, since they have very little room for expansion cards or additional drives and are more likely to suffer from overheating due to poor air circulation. Mid tower cases are typically about 7" wide by 17" high by 17" front to back, and should have at least three open 5.25" bays for such things as CD-ROM drives and two 3.5" bays for such things as floppy drives and Zip drives. In addition, there should be space inside for at least two internal hard drives. A feature that has become more common in the last year is the addition of USB ports to the front of the computer in addition to those available on the rear.

Finally, if you need more drive bays, or if you plan to stand the computer on the floor beside your desk, you may want to get a full tower case. This will probably cost $50–$100 more, but if this is what you need, then it is worth the difference. A full tower case will usually allow you to have up to five or six external drive bays that hold such things as floppies, Zip drives, CD-ROMs, **tape backup** drives, etc., in addition to four or more internal hard drives. If you expect to open the case very often, you should specify a case with a side panel that pops off easily, rather than one where you have to remove the entire outer shell.

For most users, a 250 watt **power supply** is ample. Although computers have grown much more powerful over the last 15 years, their power requirements (in terms of electricity) have not gone up at all. In fact, there has been a concerted effort to reduce the power required for computers (**Energy Star**), and in many cases, energy needs are actually much less. ATX power supplies provide options such as sleep mode, actually powering the system down when you select "shutdown" from within Windows, or powering the system up from a remote signal over a modem or network. Virtually all new computer systems now use an ATX power supply.

Even with reduced energy needs, a computer generates quite a bit of heat, so you also need to pay close attention to how well it is cooled. Cooling is usually provided by two or three fans that pull cool air from outside the case, and push hot air out the opposite corner. If the internal layout of the case is too constricted, or if the ribbon cables are poorly arranged, air flow through the case may be blocked, and the system can overheat. If the sides of the case seem to be warm to the touch, then you may need to improve the air flow through the case by rearranging cables or adding another fan.

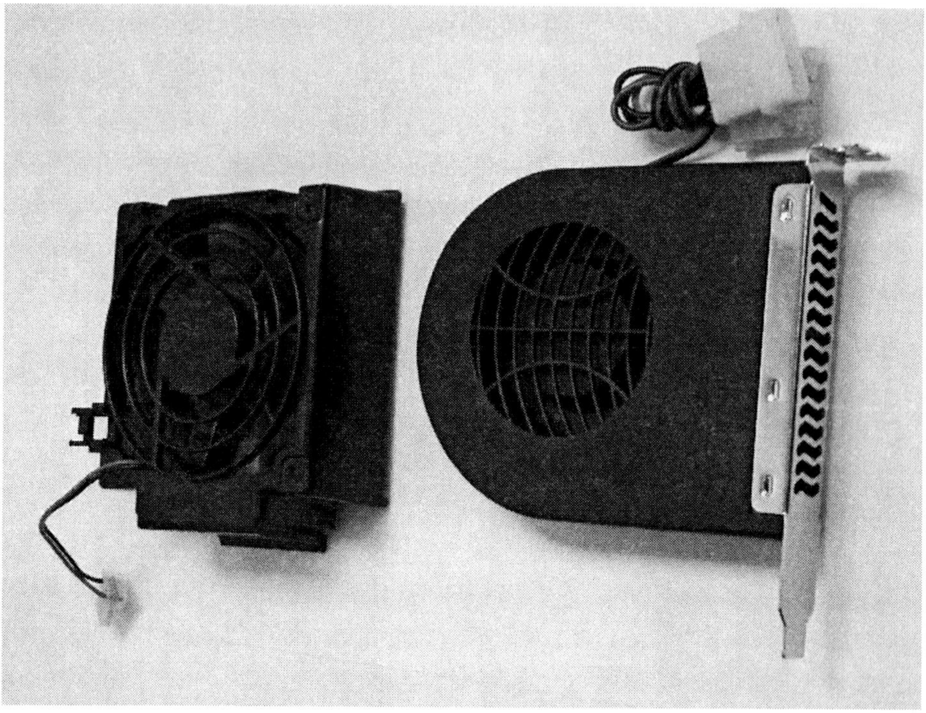

The fan on the left is typical of cooling fans found in computers, while the one on the right is a design that fits in a slot on the rear of the computer, and is advertised to pull over ten cubic feet per minute of air out of the case. It is especially good to put next to a fast video card that needs a lot of cooling.

Keyboard

Enhanced 104-key keyboard

Upgrade to Microsoft Ergonomic Keyboard add $59

All computers come with **keyboards**, but you may want to upgrade to a better model, or even buy a separate one that specifically suits you. Most keyboards sold today are of the 104-key Windows 95 pattern with the function keys along the top of the board, and separate **cursor** and numeric keypads. However, there are a lot of small differences between keyboard layouts, and individual preferences vary widely. For example, I will not use a keyboard that doesn't have a large backspace key. Other people want keyboards with an oversized <enter> key. In addition to

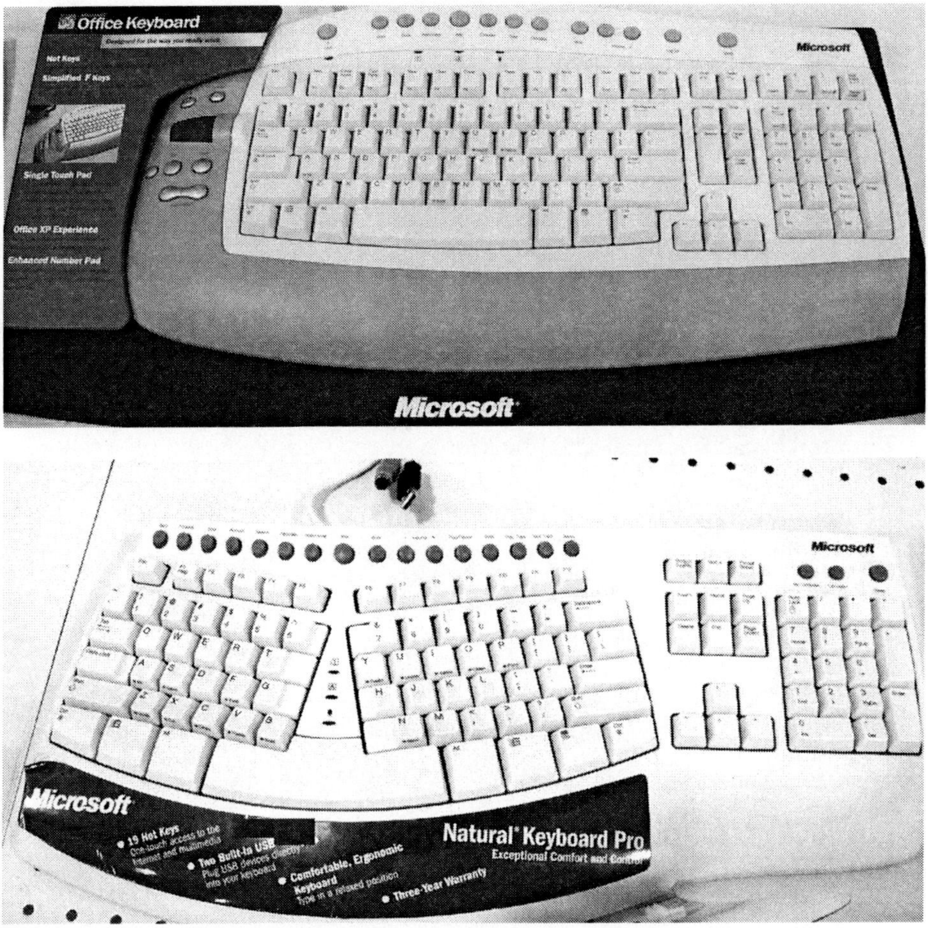

Top: **This is a standard keyboard layout, with the addition of some extra buttons along the top that can be customized according to the user's preferences. Note the USB plug. This keyboard uses only a USB port.** ***Bottom:*** **This is Microsoft's famous ergonomic keyboard. In theory the angled layout of the keys should reduce the stress of using it. Personally, I don't like to use this type of keyboard, but I know many people who do. Note the plugs at the top. This keyboard can use either a standard keyboard port or a USB port.**

the layout, the feel is very important. Some people like a keyboard that provides a "click" when keys are pressed, and others don't. For this reason, you may want to go into a computer store and try some different keyboards to find one that really suits you. After all, other than the monitor, the keyboard is the part of the computer that you will be in contact with the most.

A number of **ergonomic** keyboards are also on the market. These separate the keys used by the right and left hands and angle them together toward the top of the keyboard. Some actually have hinges and pivots so that the user can adjust each half for maximum comfort.

Mouse

Microsoft Mouse (PS/2)

Many companies make mice, but nearly all are similar in appearance. They may have two or three buttons, but this doesn't really matter, because no major application uses the middle button on a three-button **mouse**. (However, Logitech provides software with their 3-button mice that allows a single click of the middle button to replace the "double-click" that many people find difficult.) Good quality is important though, because mice pick up dirt, and are more subject to problems than most other parts of a computer. Two of the major manufacturers are Microsoft and Logitech.

Although most mice use a ball that rolls around to generate a signal to move the cursor, there are also optical mice available that have no moving parts. They use a light source that senses the motion of the mouse. This eliminates the problem of picking up dirt and lint, but they must be used on a surface that has a distinct texture. Something like a blank sheet of white paper will usually not work well as a surface for an optical mouse.

There are also mice available that use an infrared interface to elim-

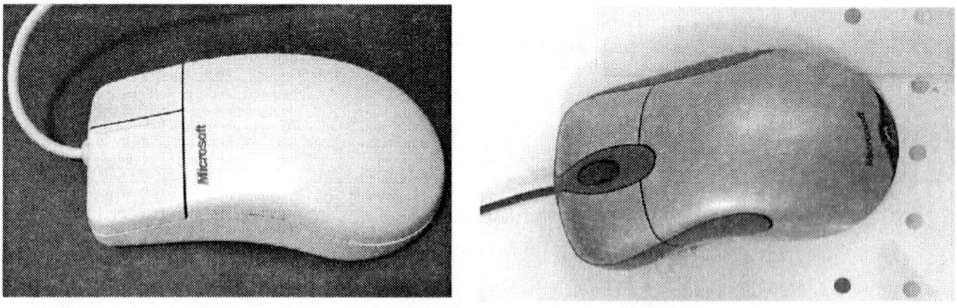

***Left:* This is a standard Microsoft mouse. There are millions of them in use around the world. *Right:* This shows the wheel between the two mouse buttons that allows rapid scrolling without moving the mouse.**

inate the need for a cord to connect the mouse to the computer. These cordless mice can be very handy, but may not be advisable if you are the kind who easily looses things, or whose kids carry things away.

Microsoft recently added an innovation that they call IntelliMouse. It includes a small roller between the mouse buttons that allows you to scroll up and down through many applications without having to move the cursor to the scroll bar. Other companies have added similar features, and which kind you get is purely a matter of choice.

Some people prefer a **trackball**, which is kind of an upside-down mouse. It is a big ball (about like a ball from a pool table) mounted in a holder with a button on each side. A big advantage to a trackball is that it can fit snugly between the end of the keyboard and the wall or books or whatever; it doesn't need any room to move.

Another pointing device that is gaining popularity is the **touch-pad**. These first became popular in portable systems, but many people also are using them on their desktop systems. There are even keyboards available that have touch-pads built in.

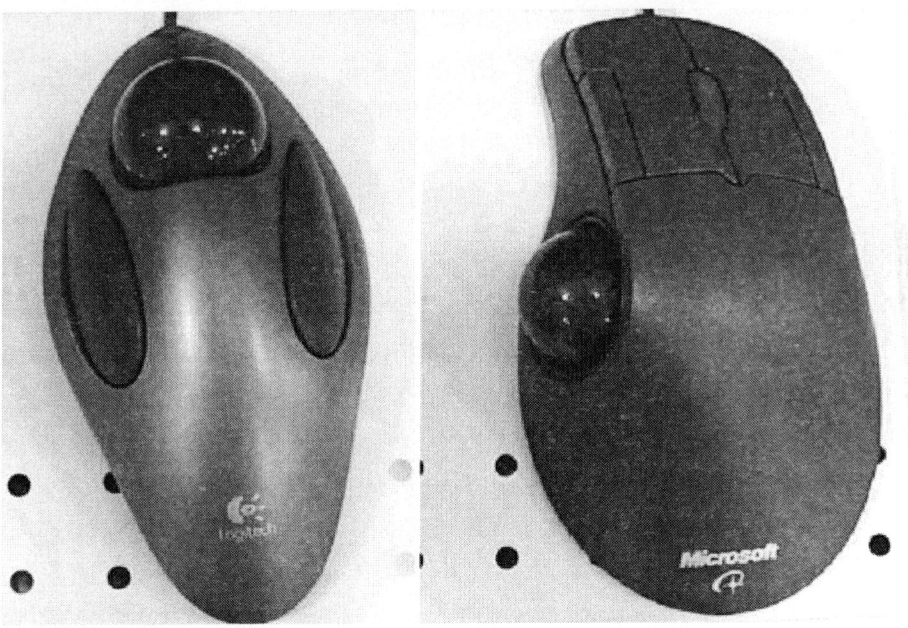

Here are two trackballs, one with the ball in the middle where it is moved with the fingers, and the other with the ball on the left where it is moved by the thumb. Note that with the ball in the middle it can be either right- or left-handed, but with the ball on the left it can only be used by the right hand.

Operating System

Windows XP Home/Microsoft Works 2003 on CD

The most common **operating system** being sold with new systems is Windows XP. However, there are still millions of users out there running earlier versions of Windows or even DOS and Windows 3.1. Windows XP is a very stable and versatile operating system, but it does have a serious annoyance from my point of view with regard to its "product activation" requirements. Microsoft has stated that this is to prevent piracy, but as often as I change the hardware in my system it can be a real pain to have to re-activate Windows XP. For most users, this will be a one-time event, however.

At the same time, I also have a system running Mandrake Linux 9.0, and while I am not ready to move everything over to it yet, it is very nice. The main shortcoming is that there are still some applications (all right, games) that I use regularly that have not yet been made available for Linux, but I hope this will change soon.

Most companies also **bundle** software with the purchase so that new users can start to use the computer right away when they set it up. The quality and value of this software should be a consideration when you buy, but don't ever take the manufacturer's word for the value of the software. Statements such as "$1400 worth of bundled software" are common, when most of it is out of date and could be purchased by the user if desired (not likely!) for less than $300. It probably cost the manufacturer less than $100. Packages such as Microsoft Office are much more valuable, but are not offered by as many dealers.

In this case, the reference to having MS Works on CD means that you would actually get the installation CD for MS works with the system, rather than just having it installed on the hard drive, with no way to recover or fix it if it later needed to be reinstalled. Always ask for installation CDs for all software included with a system.

Warranty

3-year parts/labor warranty, 1-year onsite

As with tech support, a better warranty will probably get you a better computer, but remember that a warranty is only as good as the company behind it. I would be very cautious about a company that has only been in business a few months that offers a three-year warranty. If they go out of business, then your warranty is history, and your free tech support, too. A computer company that has been in business for several years and that appears to be stable offers much better odds.

Note: Many system components, such as hard drives, monitors, CD-ROM drives, etc., are actually under warranty from the Original Equipment Manufacturer or **OEM**. Thus, if you have a Seagate hard drive that quits while under Seagate's warranty, Seagate will replace it, regardless of the status of the company you bought it from. On the other hand, some computer sellers will refer users back to the OEM for support, even if they are still in business. This can be very annoying, as it means that you have multiple points of contact for support, and getting final resolution to a problem can be more difficult.

Therefore, if you have a good system, having the company that you bought it from go out of business is only a minor inconvenience, since most computer parts are quite generic. If a part goes bad, you may have to pay to replace it, but the odds are that it won't fail during the warranty period anyway.

Some manufacturers order OEM versions of sound cards, video cards, etc., which do not have all the features or options of the regular models. Sometimes these cards are then sold at a discount on the open market, leaving buyers feeling ripped off because they didn't get the full version that appeared to be advertised.

Also, don't be impressed by longer warranties on labor from mail-order companies; the parts warranty is what counts. If you have to return a system for service after the parts warranty has expired, you will be expected to pay shipping both directions, and this will greatly outweigh local labor costs. In fact, it will almost certainly be cheaper to pay somebody local for repairs than it will be to pay the shipping to and from your original dealer. Of course, if you buy from a local dealer, then an extended labor warranty is probably a good value.

Tech Support

Toll-Free tech support for the life of your system

The importance of good tech support is often overlooked. The better a company supports its products, the less likely you are to need support, at least for repairs. A company that offers toll-free tech support over the phone, or better yet on-site tech support for at least a year, loses money whenever one of its systems breaks down, or even suffers a minor glitch. Therefore, they have a strong incentive to use high quality components, and to assemble and test them well. On the other hand, a company that offers the very lowest prices, but not even a toll-free number to call for help (or whose toll-free number is *always* busy), may well have used the cheapest available parts to build a system that is less reliable. I don't recommend buying a system from a mail-order company that doesn't offer toll-free tech support. (Many companies that provide toll-free tech support are almost impossible to reach, however. Stories of days spent in voice-mail hell trying to reach tech support are far too common.) If they offer a year of free, on-site tech support in addition, so much the better. You will pay a little more for such coverage, but in return you will probably get a much better computer, and much better support in case something does go wrong. If it is a well-established local company, then check with some of their local customers to find out how well they provide support.

E-mail support is another option that nearly all companies offer, and for minor glitches, or for informational queries, it is fine. However, if your computer is not working for any reason, then being told to e-mail them with a description of the problem can be infuriating.

You should also note, however, that some companies are now charging $35 or so for telephone tech support for software, even if it is software that they installed at the factory. Since it is often difficult for even experienced users to distinguish between hardware and software problems, a "free" tech support call can turn expensive in a hurry. Furthermore, they usually won't even talk to you until they have a credit card number, in the event that they decide that it is a software problem.

Advertising Tricks

Prices of new computers have dropped enormously over the past few years, but it is not uncommon to see advertised prices that are still well below normal market levels. This usually means that the price advertised is "after rebate", and to get the rebate you have to sign up for a three-year contract with some internet service provider (ISP), usually at a rate of $20 per month. There are less expensive ISPs out there, but even if you choose one that costs that much, you might prefer a different one than is offering the rebate. Also, since it is a three-year contract, if you decide after a few months that service stinks and you want to change, then the balance of the three-year contract comes due at once.

I recommend that you compare the price before the rebate as the real price of the system, and make your decision to purchase or not purchase on that basis. In any case, if it has been a year or more since you have last priced computers, I strongly recommend that you look at several different systems in the price range that you are considering so that you are aware of the current price range. For a quick reality check, I like to go to eBay and look at systems that are configured according to what I am looking for, even though I may not plan to buy there. But be aware that nearly all systems offered there come without an operating system, and adding Windows XP will add about $100 to the price.

Conclusion: Avoid systems that offer huge rebates for signing long-term contracts with a particular ISP. It limits your future options too much. If your needs are not great (if you don't play the latest games), then a low-end system may well meet your needs for a while, but don't get yourself locked into a contract that forces you to pay long after the value is gone.

What's It REALLY Going to Cost?

Given that the computer market evolves so quickly, it is difficult to say what a computer system should cost. As of November 2002 (as I am writing this) a good new system, such as a Pentium IV running at 2.4 GHz with 512 MB RAM, 80 GB hard drive, CD-RW, DVD-ROM, GeForce IV video card, four USB 2.0 ports, a 17" monitor, and Windows XP home should cost around $1000–$1200. If you drop the monitor and the operating system, and cut the other components back to minimum current standards, you can get a functional system for as little as $250, including 1.4 GHz CPU, 40 GB hard drive, CD-ROM drive, and integrated sound, video, and other components.

While this low-end system may be somewhat better than what you now have, and sound like a cheap upgrade, you should be aware that some applications require substantially more powerful computers than others. Word processing, e-mail, genealogy, Internet browsing, etc., do not require an especially powerful system, and nearly any system sold new today will be adequate for these applications for at least 2–3 years. However, if you want to get into desktop publishing (**DTP**), photo editing, programming, creating multimedia content, **CAD**, or playing the latest computer games, then you should look for a system that is close to the high end available at the time you make your purchase.

Summary Checklist

CPU—At the low end, a Celeron or AMD Duron at 1.4 GHz or faster. For most users, a Pentium IV or Athlon XP system is recommended.

RAM—256 MB minimum, and most users should get at least 512 MB.

Hard Drive—Even on a tight budget, get at least a 40 GB hard drive, since you save almost nothing by getting a smaller one.

Floppy Drive—Get a 3.5", 1.44 MB floppy drive.

CD-ROM—Get an 24× or faster drive and a sound card. A DVD-ROM is a nice upgrade, as is a CD-RW. Heck, get both.

Removable storage—The Iomega Zip Drive is recommended over tape drives. If you need higher capacities, a CD-RW or even a DVD-RAM would be options.

Video card—AGP 3D accelerated video card with at least 32 MB RAM.

Monitor—Non-interlaced at all resolutions, dot pitch 0.31 mm or less, 15" to 19".

Fax/Modem—56K.

Mouse—Your call. Easily replaced if you don't like it.

Operating System—Windows XP unless you want something else.

Warranty—Minimum one year, lots of places now offer 2 or 3 year parts warranties.

Tech Support—Don't even consider a company that doesn't provide toll-free (or local) tech support for as long as you have the system.

Don't forget that you will almost certainly need a printer with your computer, and at current prices you may want to get a scanner as well. You can read about these items in Chapter 5.

4

PORTABLE SYSTEMS

Some of the purchasing decisions that relate to portable systems (**laptops, notebooks, subnotebooks, tablets, handhelds**, etc.) are similar or identical to those for desktop systems, but many are not. Unless you are quite familiar with computer components, it would probably be helpful to at least scan through Chapter 3, if you have not already done so. It should also be noted that the August issue of *PC Magazine* traditionally covers portable computing, with extensive background, portable computing tips and tricks, and reviews of dozens of different systems.

Components that portable and stationary systems have in common include the **CPU**, **RAM**, and **hard** and **floppy drives**. Components that differ substantially include the **monitor** or screen, the **keyboard**, the **mouse** or pointing device, the **case**, and the **power supply**. All of these are addressed in this chapter, because even those that are similar can have differences that are significant.

Until a few years ago, manufacturers tried to distinguish between various sizes of portable systems by referring to them as laptops (larger and heavier), notebooks (in the middle) and subnotebooks (lightest but also least features). Today, however, nearly all portable systems are referred to as notebook computers, and you have to evaluate the details of the individual system to determine where in this range it falls. It helps, of course, that the capabilities of notebook computers have also increased dramatically in recent years.

This is a full-featured laptop with almost all features that you would expect to find in a laptop system, except of course, for light weight.

CPU

Although many portable systems are still in use that use older CPUs of some sort, nearly all the new ones use the **Celeron** or **Pentium IV**, although some are now coming out that use the new AMD

Mobile Athlon XP. Portable CPUs are now nearly all "voltage-reducing," meaning that they can adjust their speed (and thus the power consumed) based on the demands of the application, and whether the system is running on batteries, or is plugged into a wall socket. Reduced voltage reduces the heat generated by the chips, and extends the battery life, both of which are very important in portable systems. Even so, the "hot spot" on the bottom of a portable system can become quite uncomfortable when holding one of these systems on your lap for a prolonged period.

For now, Pentium IV mobile CPUs are available in speeds up to 2.2 **GHz**, which is right at double what was available a year ago, and faster ones are on the way. Likewise, the fastest Mobile Athlon XP CPU is the 2200, meaning that it is comparable to the 2.2 GHz P4 in performance, although it actually runs a little slower than that. These speeds provide performance that is a little slower than the latest desktop systems, but that is still substantially better than the majority of systems in use, and is adequate for virtually any computing need. And these mobile variants of the standard CPUs are designed to minimize energy use and maximize battery life, although typical systems are still limited to 2–3 hours of use at best before you need to change batteries or find a plug. The Macintosh Powerbook portables use a variant of the G4 CPU that is used in their desktop systems.

Cache

Nearly all portable systems now come with an external **cache** (also called **L2**) built in to the CPU. It will be there whether the system specifications call it out or not. Of course, if you are looking at an older used system, it may or may not be included.

RAM

Most portable systems come with 128 to 512 **MB** of **RAM**, although at the high end some have 1GB or more. If you are planning to run any current version of Windows, you should get at least 128 MB, and 256 MB is probably a worthwhile investment.

Hard Drive

While most desktop systems now come with a minimum of a 40 GB **hard drive**, portables now usually start at 20 GB, and are readily available up to 60 GB or more. Hard drives used in portables are usually about the size of a deck of cards, and it is hard to squeeze more storage into such a small package. Of course, miracles of miniaturization are being worked here too, and hard drive capacities are growing rapidly, even as the physical size continues to shrink. For most people, portable hard drives are now large enough that disk space is not a problem, but if it is, **disk compression** is still an option. (The Appendix discusses disk compression in more detail.)

Floppy Drive

Notebook computers that weigh more than 5 pounds will usually have a 3.5" floppy drive built in, while those that are less than about 5 pounds will have an external floppy drive that you can choose to either carry or leave behind. A number of systems also have a removable floppy such that an extra battery can be added in its place, while others have a single bay that can take a floppy drive, a CD-ROM drive, an extra battery, or even a **Zip** drive. However, the floppy can almost always be attached externally when one of the other drives is in the bay, so that both can be active at once.

CD-ROM and Multimedia

Nearly all notebooks now include a CD-ROM drive, although in some cases it shares a drive bay with the floppy drive. In these systems, you get both a floppy and a CD-ROM, but you can only have one installed at a time. And of course, there are some laptops with everything. Typically, the lighter systems forgo extra drives in order to save on weight. Although it costs a little more, an option that is popular in notebook systems is a combination CD-RW/DVD drive. The CD-RW is valuable because it gives an easy way to back up files from the computer, and the DVD drive is nice because it lets you choose which movies you want to watch whenever you are traveling. You can rent movies of your choice and watch them on your laptop. Of course, it still reads CDs just fine.

Nearly all portable systems now include a built-in sound card and speakers, although the sound quality is usually what you would expect from 1" speakers.

Video

Video on portable systems has improved tremendously over the last few years. Although some **dual scan passive matrix (DSTN)** color screens are still found on older used systems, nearly all portable systems now on the market use an **active matrix (TFTN)** color screen that is much brighter and easier to read. All but the smallest portables have moved away from the standard VGA resolution of 640 × 480, as screens that support 800 × 600 (**SVGA**), 1024 × 768 (**XGA**), and higher are becoming common. One of the most obvious improvements is that the screen size is now usually at least 12" from corner to corner, and can be as large as 15", which is functionally almost equivalent to a 17" desktop monitor. A few years ago screens with less than 10" diagonal measurements were common.

The Dell Latitude pictured at the beginning of this chapter has a 15.1" screen with a resolution of 1600 × 1200. This makes for a very sharp screen that shows fine details very well, but the drawback is that the characters on the screen are so tiny that many people have trouble seeing them. There are options in Windows for using larger default fonts, but a lot of programs use their own font settings, and it is not uncommon to have it display text that is too small for most people to read comfortably.

One other difference between flat-screen monitors and desktop CRT monitors is that a flat-screen monitor is designed for a specific resolution (800 × 600 or 1024 × 768, etc.), and will not run at all at a higher resolution. Lower resolutions, such as VGA (640 × 480) can be displayed by making two or more **pixels** do the job of one, but the resultant output is often ugly and hard to read.

Most portable systems have an external video outlet so you can attach an external monitor to your portable. If you have one location where you often work, it may be worth leaving a monitor there, unless you are happy with the laptop screen.

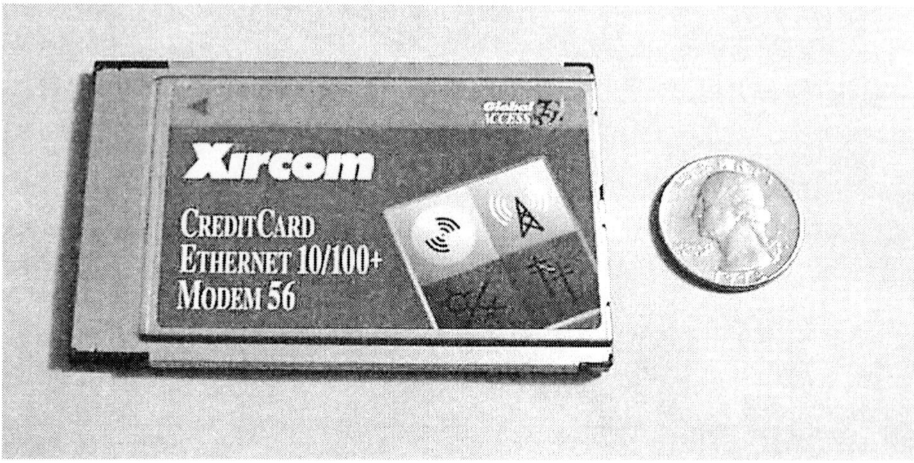

This is a combo card that combines a 56K modem and a 10/100 network card. As you can see, it is about the size of a credit card.

PC Cards and Fax/Modems

Most portable systems today come with a **PC Card** slot (**PCMCIA** was its old name) that accepts two Type II or one Type III PC Cards, which are about the size of a credit card. Type II cards (5.5 mm thick) include **fax/modems, network** cards, **SCSI** controllers, and memory cards, while most Type III cards (10.5 mm thick) are miniature hard drives. Many portable systems come with fax/modems built in, but if yours doesn't, you may want to carry a PC Card fax/modem to check e-mail or log on to on-line services while away from home.

Serial and Parallel Ports

Most portable systems come with one serial port and one parallel port. A few also have a game port, but portable systems are rarely used as serious gaming machines, so most users don't miss the game port. They do have USB ports, however, so if you want to play games on your notebook computer, shop around and pick up the controller of your choice that uses the USB port.

Case

The case is an integral part of a portable system. Since portable systems are exposed to bangs and bumps, the case needs to be strong and rigid to protect the insides. As portables have moved to larger screens, this tradeoff has become more critical, since the screens are fragile and very expensive. You don't want to carry unnecessary weight, but on the other hand, you absolutely don't want a broken screen. To keep the weight down, however, some manufacturers resort to a more flimsy case. I can't tell you what the best mix is for you, but be sensitive to this trade-off when selecting a new portable.

Keyboard

The **keyboard** is one of the least satisfactory parts of many portables. If the system is less than 11 inches wide, then the keys have been shrunk at least marginally to make them fit. If you are a touch typist, this makes it much harder to type accurately and rapidly. This is not usually a problem on the newer systems, since the larger screens make available enough room for a comfortable keyboard, but if you are looking at an older system, or one of the smallest lightweight systems, check out the keyboard carefully. You will probably use it more than you expect to, and it can be very frustrating to find that your touch-typing skills leave you with constant errors.

The feel of portable keyboards is often less satisfactory as well, because the keys are much flatter, and have very little travel. Whereas on a normal desktop keyboard the keys may be depressed several millimeters, they will probably move only 1–2 mm on a portable system, which gives very little tactile feedback. The numeric keypad is embedded in the letters, and requires a function key to activate. In any case, make sure that there are separate **cursor** keys in the standard inverted T layout. Most portable systems will also allow you to attach a full-size computer keyboard, and like an external monitor, this is probably a good idea if you have one location where you often work.

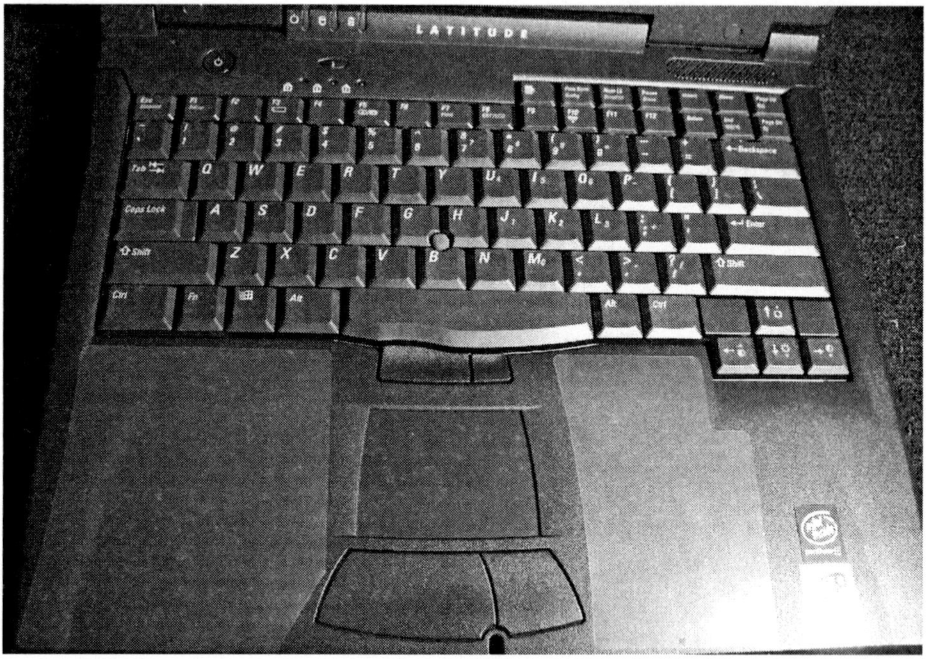

This keyboard has both a touchpad and a Trackpoint built in.

Mouse or Pointing Device

Several years ago most portable systems required you to attach a **mouse** or **trackball** if you wanted something other than keyboard input. All portables now include integral pointing devices, either a **touchpad**, or a "**Trackpoint**" that is embedded somewhere on the keyboard. IBM initiated the use of the Trackpoint on its Thinkpad systems, and it works quite well, even though it is not as fast or accurate as a regular mouse. It does have the advantage of not requiring you to move your fingers from the keyboard, since it sits at the junction of the G, H, and B keys. Deciding which of these to get is purely a matter of personal preference. At the same time, if you prefer a regular mouse, it is easy to plug one in, and can make life much more pleasant.

I personally prefer the touchpad when using a notebook computer, as dragging my finger across the pad seems more intuitive and comfortable than the Trackpoint. However, if I am using the system for any length of time, I will try to find and connect a real mouse, as the other options are just not as convenient, in my opinion.

Docking Station

Many portable systems include a docking station as an option. A **docking station** gives your portable system many of the benefits of a regular desktop computer. It always stays in your office (or home), and can be connected to a network, as well as supporting a full-sized keyboard, a full-sized monitor, and often additional hard drive or CD-ROM drive storage and/or backup. It is very convenient, since you simply slide the portable into place, and it automatically connects to the docking station. A lesser version of a docking station is called a port replicator, meaning that it allows you to make one connection that connects everything else. However, a port replicator usually does not include a monitor stand.

Operating System

Nearly all portable systems on the market today have been configured with sufficient power to run Windows XP or Windows 2000, as long as they have at least 128 MB of RAM. Although Windows 98 and Windows ME used to be the standard operating systems for portable systems, 2000 and XP are far better choices. Both versions support much better plug and play capability than the earlier versions, as well as having numerous options included specifically for portable systems.

Warranty and Tech Support

Warranties on portable systems rarely exceed a year, and on-site tech support is also rare. Instead, a few companies provide next-day replacement service anywhere in the United States if a system fails. Most still offer an 800 number where you can call for tech support, but usually the systems must be returned to the dealer if they need repair.

AC Adapters and Batteries

Almost all portable systems include **AC adapters** and batteries. The batteries are recharged by plugging in the AC adapter, and most systems can be operated without a battery when the AC adapter is plugged in. Pay attention to the size of the adapter. Some are very small and weigh only a few ounces; others are larger, and may weigh a couple of pounds. Rather than figuring on just the weight of the portable, you should include everything that you need to carry along to get the travel weight, and the AC adapter contributes significantly to this. Of course, if you have a docking station at your destination, you may not need to carry the AC adapter, since nearly all docking stations can also recharge the portable.

Batteries also contribute a lot to the weight of a system, as well as determining how long it will run while away from an AC adapter. Nearly all batteries today are **lithium ion,** although some of the lower-end systems still use **nickel metal hydride**, or **NiMH**. NiMH batteries are heavier and tend to wear out more quickly, losing their ability to hold a charge. Although most computers use rechargeable batteries, one exception is that some of the smallest handheld units use standard AA alkaline batteries, and have no provision to use AC power. You simply buy more batteries and replace them whenever they are worn out.

Carrying Cases

With nearly every portable system, you will get a carrying case of some sort. Usually these are made of nylon, with adequate padding to protect the computer from the normal bumps and jolts of hauling them around. However, by paying extra you can find carrying cases that cater to a variety of needs, from shiny leather ones that proclaim your status, to backpack cases that may be more popular with students. Essential features of any case, in addition to protection for the computer, include space to carry add-on equipment such as extra drives, AC adapter, cables, mouse, disks, etc.

Handheld Systems/PDAs/Tablets

Little mention was made in this chapter about **handheld** systems, but this is a rapidly growing segment of the market. The Palm Pilot is very popular, but it has numerous competitors. One of the problems

Here are two carrying cases for a laptop. The one on the left is a backpack, while the one on the right is like a more traditional soft-sided briefcase.

with making any recommendations in this area is that the needs of users and the variety of options on systems both vary so widely that it is hard to make any generalizations. If you are not a touch typist, then one of the mini keyboards found on larger handhelds may be adequate, especially if you need access to e-mail but not much else as you travel. If you prefer to use handwriting recognition, then the Palm Pilot, or one of its **clones** that has no keyboard at all may be preferable.

For the ultra-connected, a handheld system (like the Palm VII) that incorporates wireless technology means that you never need to worry about not being able to stay in touch, but the cost is not for the budget-

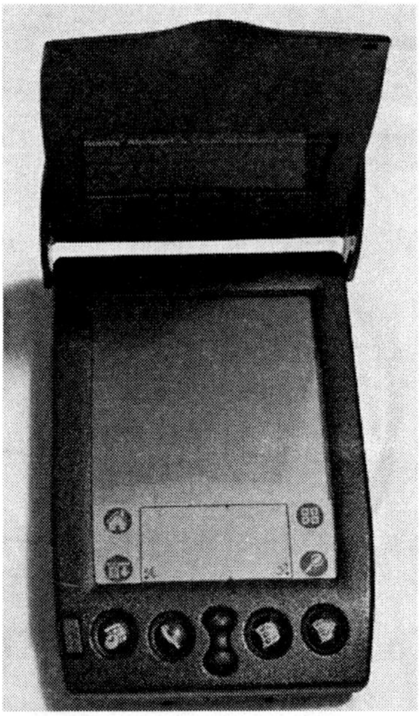

Palmpilot

minded. On the other hand, wireless connectivity is growing rapidly, and may soon be a "must have" feature in all of our computing equipment.

Ultimately, I don't expect to buy a **PDA** until one is built that incorporates a decent version of voice recognition. When I am able to simply reach up and press a lapel button (visions of Star Trek) and speak to my computer, to make appointments, set reminders, make phone calls, etc., and have it likewise communicate with me, then I will be ready to make the investment.

Tablet computers have been in use for specialized applications, such as hospitals, delivery services, etc., for several years, but Microsoft has just introduced a tablet computer version of Windows XP, and several companies are selling tablet computers that run it. I have read about them, but have not yet seen one or had a chance to play with it, so I can't say a lot so far. For many uses and users, however, it looks like it may be a very popular product.

5

PRINTERS, SCANNERS, AND OTHER STUFF

In addition to computers per se, this chapter discusses some of the **peripheral** items that many people need. These include **printers, plotters, scanners, digital cameras, surge protectors, uninterruptible power supplies, USB pen drives**, and other odds and ends.

Printers

Most printers sold today fall into one of two categories, either **inkjet** or **laser**. Below is a discussion of the pros and cons of each. For more details and reviews of many printers, PC Magazine's Annual Printer Issue, published each November, is an invaluable resource.

INKJET

Nearly all inkjet printers on the market today have at least the option of printing in color. At the low end are printers that require you to insert a black-ink cartridge for black printing, and a three-color cartridge for color printing. These printers start as low as $40 and can produce black and white text pages that are almost as good as a laser printer, but their color output is usually not so good. There are also inkjet printers in this range that do not require you to swap cartridges for color or black printing.

This is an Epson Stylus C60 color inkjet printer, which is advertised as printing up to 12 pages per minute of text, and is priced at $79.95 after rebate. While this model may be discontinued by the time you read this, comparable models will be available.

For $100 and up, you can get color inkjet printers that produce stunning color images as well. In some cases, these are nearly as good as photographs, although special paper is usually required for the sharpest output. If you expect to do much color printing, pay very close attention to the cost of ink. While inkjet printers are quite inexpensive, the cost of ink cartridges can add up very quickly, and paying a little more for a printer that has a lower cost-per-page for printing is often a good move. A few color inkjet printers use a combination of colors to make black, for common text. Avoid these in favor of a printer that uses a true black ink for black printing.

A few months ago I needed to get a new printer, and I found one on a close-out sale at $40, but when I priced ink cartridges for it, they were over $20 each. When I got home I searched on the Internet and found **clone** ink cartridges for this model of printer for less than $5, so I went back and bought the printer. The warranty warned against using anything but brand-name cartridges, but I decided that if the printer quit I could throw it away and get another one for less than the cost of replacing both the color and black ink cartridges. So far I have not had any problems, and I have worked through at least three black cartridges and one color one since I bought it. In any case, it is obvious that many companies are virtually giving away inkjet printers, and hoping to make their profits selling ink.

Print quality for the various inkjet printers is usually fairly good when printing text, even at the low end, but the real difference is that by paying a little more for a printer, you can usually get one that prints much more photo realistic images.

Laser Printers

The laser printer is the workhorse of the modern office. The least expensive of these prints clear text at 600 **dpi** and 6–12 pages per minute and costs under $200. As the price goes up from here, printers get sharper output, up to 1200 × 1200 dpi, network connections so that multiple computers can share the printer over the network, larger paper trays, duplex printing that can print both sides without manual intervention, and larger toner cartridges that don't need to be replaced so often. As with inkjet printers, the less expensive laser printers usually have a much higher cost per page when you figure in the cost of toner. Of course, if you don't print more than 100 pages per month or so, this may still be the way to go, but if you print a lot more than that, figure the total cost to own and operate it for a period of two or more years, based on your anticipated usage rates. Regardless of which speed or resolution you get, if you need to print full-page graphic images, make sure that it comes with at least 8 MB of RAM. This may boost the price a few dollars, but the images will not print completely without enough RAM.

This is a low-end laser printer listed at $200, but it still prints 600 dpi images at 12 pages per minute.

Color laser printers are also becoming more common, with a few models selling for less than $1000. Most color laser printers still sell for something between $1000 and $4000, though, and there are not really any of them that are yet priced and configured to be suitable for a home environment. Instead, they are designed and intended for office environments, where several users will share a color printer for those jobs

This is a more capable laser printer that lists at $500, but can print up to 16 ppm at 1200 dpi, print duplex (both sides), and be shared over a network.

that require color. Also, don't expect to get true color photographs from a laser printer. Some are much better than others, and nearly all are good enough for presentation graphics or producing a newsletter, but a good color inkjet printer will usually have sharper, clearer colors and produce an image that is closer to photo-realistic.

THERMAL WAX

Thermal wax printers are high-end color printers. If you are producing color graphics for business presentations or advertising purposes,

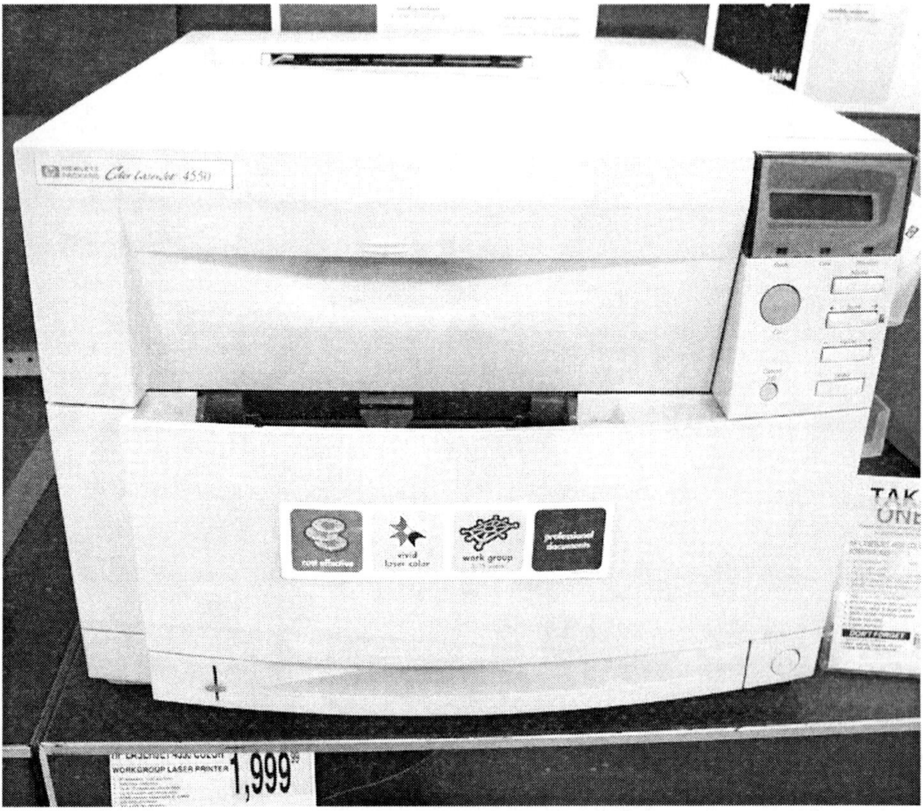

This is a Hewlett Packard Laser Jet 4550 color laser printer, listed at $2000. I use these at work, and they are great printers.

then you can probably justify one of these printers. Thermal wax transfer printers ($1000–$3000) have sharp, vivid colors, but don't blend the colors into photo-realistic images. For graphic art, charts, diagrams, etc., they are usually fine, and almost always have brighter colors than a color laser, but if you want to edit color photographs and produce images that are indistinguishable from original 35-mm photographs, you will have to get a thermal wax diffusion printer, often called a dye sublimation printer. These printers range from $1000–$15,000, but can produce images that are indistinguishable from 35-mm photographs. The major differences between the various printers in this class relate to the size paper they can print on, and the speed with which they print.

If all you want to do is print out photographs in a 4" × 6" format or smaller, then there are small printers that are designed specifically to do this, and for only a few hundred dollars. However, the cost of ink and paper may still be higher than for developing normal pictures, although the freedom that they provide to use a digital camera, and edit the photos on your computer before printing, may make the cost a secondary issue.

PLOTTERS

Most **plotters** sold today use the same print heads that are used in the inkjet printers described earlier, but do it on a much larger scale. Plotters can print on paper anywhere from 17" × 22" to 48" × 150'. They are used for printing architectural and engineering drawings, large spreadsheets, or Gantt charts. If you need to print any of these, then a plotter is really your only choice. As a bonus, virtually all inkjet plotters will produce excellent color output, since color print heads are now standard.

There are some older pen plotters on the market, some at very cut-rate prices, but their resolution is much worse than inkjets, and they usually won't print the **True-type** or **Postscript** fonts that are almost universally used by today's programs. For these reasons, I don't recommend pen plotters.

Scanners

Scanners take images or text on paper and convert them into an electronic format that a computer can use. They come in one of two formats: As flat-bed units in which the paper is placed face down on the glass bed of the scanner, and the scanner head under the glass scans the image from the paper into the computer, or as pull-through units where the sheet of paper is pulled through the scanner as the image is scanned.

There are several functional differences between these two types of scanner. The pull-through design is more compact, but thicker paper, such as photographs, may not pass through well, and the pull-through mechanism can mangle sheets if they get started crooked or are fragile, and of course, pages from a book or magazine cannot be scanned without tearing out the page.

This is a flat-bed scanner, on which you place the page you want to scan, and then close the cover to hold it still.

Flat-bed scanners hold the paper against a glass plate (just like a copier), while moving the scanning mechanism across the page, and just as with a copier, it is possible to fold open a book or magazine and scan pages without damage to the volume. Flat-bed color scanners start at as little as $50 and up, although more expensive units provide a number of features that are lacking on the low-end units, such as faster scans, larger formats, automatic page feeders, more accurate color recognition, and higher resolutions.

A few of the low end scanners plug into the parallel port of the computer, although scanners that use the USB port are rapidly replacing them. If you have a choice between parallel and USB interfaces, get the USB, assuming you have a computer that has a USB port and that you are running Windows 98 or later. Most high-end scanners connect to a SCSI controller, since this allows higher scanning speeds.

Most scanners are offered with a variety of software packages for editing images or **OCR** (optical character recognition), allowing you to convert paper documents into text files that you can then edit on your word processor.

Combo Unit

Another option that is gaining market share is the combination printer/fax/scanner/copier. It combines all these functions into a single unit, saving desk space (and money, assuming that you would otherwise have bought separate units for each of these functions). If you need most or all of these functions, then a combo unit can be a good

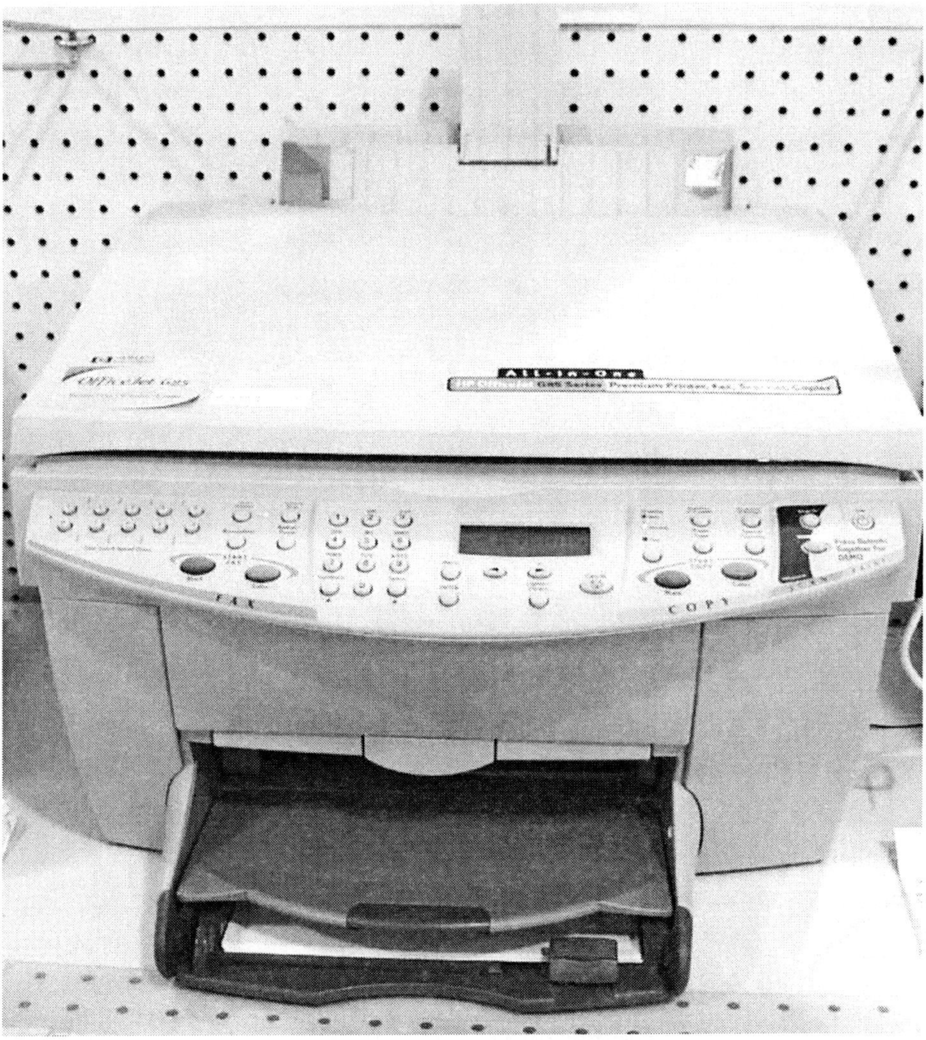

This is a Hewlett Packard G85 combo unit.

deal. Some use inkjet technology, and some use laser technology, and the majority use pull-through technology, rather than flat-bed scanner technology, which can be a limitation for some people. And of course, if one part of the unit develops problems, then you lose the use of the whole unit while it is being repaired. This is one instance where I would have a strong preference for buying from a reputable and well-established local vendor.

I have also found that models that were sold a year or more ago often do not have drivers for the latest operating systems. Apparently the manufacturers are unwilling to pay their programmers to update the drivers, which are then posted for free on the Internet. Instead, they want to push people to buy a new unit. This problem is worse for the combo units than for printers or scanners in general, apparently because the drivers have to be more complex in order to support all the different functions.

Digital Cameras

The price of digital cameras has dropped to as little as $50–$100 for low-end units, and their use is exploding. Even a low-end camera is good enough to take pictures for a personal web site, and graphics really jazz up a page. Picture quality improves as the price rises, with **megapixel** cameras now available for under $100 for some models. Digital cameras with up to 5-megapixel resolution are available, although the cost rises in rough proportion to the resolution. Even with the high-end cameras, resolution is not as good as with a good 35-mm film camera, but the differences will not be visible to most users unless the image is blown up to 8 × 10 inches or larger. Of course, in addition to the megapixel rating, other features such as a zoom lens, the amount of memory included, the ability to take macro (up close) pictures, and a variety of other options also greatly influence the price.

One of the big advantages to a digital camera is that the cost per picture to display images on your computer is zero, if you don't count the cost of the camera itself (printing them out can cost as much as regular photo developing, however), and pictures can be transmitted by e-mail to friends and co-workers. With image-editing software, kids of all ages can have fun doing all sorts of strange things to pictures of anyone or anything.

I have a digital camera, and I have found that one of the nicest features is that I take a lot more experimental or "play" pictures, since I don't have to worry about the cost of film or developing. I simply import the images to my computer, and then keep those that I really like. A lot of them are no good, but then they didn't cost me anything either. I would recommend that you get as much memory as the camera can hold, so that you don't find yourself limited to just a few pictures before you have to erase some.

This is my camera. This model is no longer in production, but comparable models are readily available.

The Kodak DC4800 shown here is my personal camera. It came originally with a 16 MB **Compact Flash** card, which is good for about 16 pictures at the highest resolution. However, I purchased an additional 256 MB Compact Flash card that lets me take over 250 pictures before I run out of memory. Actually, I have found that a 2 megapixel image (1800 × 1200) is ample for nearly everything that I do, and at that resolution, I can take almost 350 pictures on my Compact Flash card. For me, this camera has really put the fun back in photography, since I can take all the pictures I want and view them as soon as I get to my computer, all at no cost for film or developing. All the pictures in this book were taken with this camera.

Surge Suppressers

This surge suppresser has two plugs at the lower end designed for the little AC adapter boxes that so often block adjacent plugs. This is a nice feature to consider when buying a surge suppresser.

Although they don't happen every day, voltage spikes in the electricity coming into your computer can fry electrical components. For this reason, most people buy a surge suppresser to filter out any spikes that might hit. Most surge suppressers come in one of two forms; the less expensive ones look like a six-outlet power strip while the more expensive are platforms about 1.5" thick and a foot square that sit under the monitor. The latter have several switches on the front so you can turn off individual components such as printers or monitors, as well as a master switch that turns everything on and off at once. Many surge suppressers of both types also have telephone jacks built in to protect your system from any surges that might come in through your phone line (if you are using a modem).

Regardless of which type surge suppresser you choose, don't go without. It makes sense to spend $10–$80 on a surge suppresser to protect the thousands of dollars you have invested in your computer. Caution: One significant voltage spike can destroy the ability of the surge suppresser to protect from future spikes, so you probably want to replace it any time you suspect a serious spike has hit.

UPSs

A surge suppresser will protect you against electrical spikes, but they do nothing about the power dips or flickers that are common in

This gives a little feel for the options and variety that are available in UPSs. In general, you only need one of the larger ones if you have a 19" or larger monitor on your system.

many areas. A brief loss of power that just causes lights to flicker will often cause a computer to reset, wiping out any work that has not been saved to disk. Since this can be annoying in any case, and sometimes catastrophic, **UPS**s (uninterruptible power supplies) are used on many systems to provide power to the computer even when the lights go out. They usually have power sufficient for only 20 minutes or less, but this is still plenty of time to save work in progress and do a graceful shutdown. And in the case of power fluctuations that make the lights flicker, the computer keeps right on working. All UPSs include protection against electrical spikes so there is no need to have both a surge suppresser and a UPS on your system, although you may want to put a surge suppresser in front of a UPS to protect the UPS from spikes. UPSs adequate for a single PC cost anywhere from $100 on up.

Note: A laser printer should never be plugged into a UPS, as laser printers draw far more current than any home UPS can provide.

Compact Flash Cards/Reader

If you have one or more devices that use **Compact Flash** cards, such as digital cameras, **MP3** players, digital recorders, etc., you may find it convenient to add a Compact Flash reader to your system. Nearly all such units simply plug into the USB port, and do not require any other power source. Despite usually being referred to as readers, they both read and write data from Compact Flash Cards.

The Compact Flash (often written as CompactFlash) cards themselves are becoming very common for applications where light weight (they weigh less than an ounce) and durability (they have no moving parts) are important. Data stored in them is **nonvolatile**, meaning that even if the power is turned off and the card is removed from its parent device, it will maintain its data, at least for as long as it is protected from excessive heat, magnets, etc. For now, the maximum capacity for Compact Flash cards is 512 MB, but that will almost certainly continue to increase.

Compact Flash type memory is now being attached to a USB plug

This is a 16 MB card, but cards in this format are available up to 512 MB or larger.

such that you can simply plug it into a USB port and copy files to and from the device. These are usually referred to as either **pen drives** or **memory keys**. The memory key refers to the fact that many of these are small enough to fit on a key chain, while nearly any of them will fit fine into a shirt pocket or purse. Capacities range from 8 MB to 512 MB or more, and they currently cost about $0.50 per MB for those in the 32 to 256 MB range.

This Compact Flash reader makes it much simpler to transfer data to and from a device that uses the CF cards.

Home Networking

The number of home **networks** is growing very rapidly. The primary reason is that many homes now have more than one computer,

This is a little network minihub that can allow up to eight computers or other network devices to connect to each other.

and there are resources that users of the various computers want to share, such as a high-speed internet connection, printers, or even just access to each other for networked games.

There are a variety of ways to set up a home network. Being the computer jock that I am, I opted to use traditional network cards in each computer, connected through a **mini-hub** and **Cat-5** network cable. This has the advantage of using standard, inexpensive components, and is very fast and reliable, but running the wires was a real challenge. If you have a phone outlet near each computer, network hardware is available that will let you use your existing phone lines to network your computers. However, for most homes the best solution is probably a wireless network that uses a low-power radio signal to let the computers talk to each other. Typically, these are not as fast as wired networks, but they are certainly fast enough to keep up with most internet connections, and they are usually very easy to install and configure.

6

SOFTWARE

Although most of this book talks about how to decide what hardware to buy, the real reason to buy the hardware is to get access to the capabilities of **software**. Simply stated, software is the general term for programs that you run on the computer, whether word processing, spreadsheet, art, database, Internet browser, games, etc.

Which types of programs you will get depends on your needs and interests, and indeed, rudimentary versions of all the above except the spreadsheet and database are included with Windows. (Wordpad, Paint, HyperTerminal, Solitaire, and Minefield. Internet Explorer is hardly rudimentary.) Wordpad, for example, is a better word processor than anything that was on the market before 1986 or so, and is *much* better than the word processor that I used to write my master's thesis in 1984. At the same time, Microsoft's Word for Windows 97, used to write this book, adds so many capabilities and tools, and at such a reasonable price, that there is no reason for me to make do with less. On the other hand, Word XP, part of Office XP, has been out for several months, and I use it at work, but for home use, it simply doesn't add enough value, for what I do, to be worth the cost of the upgrade.

Several years ago the price for major brands of common software plummeted, especially if you purchased a **suite** that included a word processor, a spreadsheet, presentation graphics, and possibly a database. The competition between Microsoft, Lotus, and WordPerfect resulted in much lower prices for the end user. However, now that Microsoft has over 90 percent of the market, prices for their office suite have gone back up quite a lot. If you are willing to be a little different, you can still get a great office suite from Corel, who bought the WordPerfect suite, for about a third or less of what the Microsoft Office suite costs. In fact, there are many companies that include the WordPerfect suite with every new computer that they sell.

If compatibility with most other users is a primary concern, then you will probably want to invest in the Microsoft Office suite, although other office suites feature the ability to read and write to the Microsoft file formats. If, on the other hand, you are primarily working on your own, without extensive collaboration with others, then any product that does the job will be adequate, and that means just about any suite on the market for most of us.

I would strongly recommend, however, that you not **bootleg** or pirate (make unauthorized copies of) software. Make do with the stuff included with Windows for a while if you have to, or buy close-out copies of older versions of Word, WordPerfect, Excel, Lotus, etc. that are being sold at clearance prices. Actually, these programs are still excellent, and more than adequate for nearly all uses. Also, you can sometimes use them to buy the current versions at the upgrade price, and thus save yourself some money.

Another option is to get a lower-end integrated suite like Microsoft Works (less than $50 if you shop around), which is still more capable than software that was considered top-of-the-line a few years ago, and which now includes Word as its word processing component.

There are many other categories of software as well. If you like maps, Street Atlas USA shows every street and road in the United States. There are a variety of scriptures on CD with all sorts of supplemental commentary, all of which is searchable by key word. There are recipe databases that allow you to search for recipes by ingredient, or that avoid key ingredients (very useful for people with food sensitivities). There are genealogy programs that help you keep track of all of your ancestors (you still have to identify them) and where they all fit in. Photo editing software allows you to clean up old pictures, or to produce every conceivable image manipulation. Voice recognition allows you to talk to your computer and have it understand you. There are even counseling programs that can emulate a therapist or psychiatrist (with all the usual cautions about not depending on them if you need real human help).

And of course, there are games. There have been literally tens of thousands of games written for the PC, and many of them are still on the market, or available as shareware. While the latest games require a fairly high end system, there are many games available that were written for hardware that was current ten years ago or more, and that still run fine. Most educational software for children is in the form of games, where they need to read or do basic math, or whatever, in order to complete the game. There are some people that never play any games on a computer, but they are a small minority. From those who just play an occasional game of Solitaire or FreeCell, to those who avidly seek out and play the latest fully 3D, multiplayer shooter games, or who love the mystery and ambience of Myst and its successors, games have become a leading category of software.

And finally, before we leave this section, there is software that serves only to help service and maintain the computer and its software. Into this category fall such programs as Norton Utilities, McAfee Utilities, and many others. Everybody who wants to keep their computer running smoothly should install and use at least one of these programs. (And anybody who does not care if their computer has problems needs some of that analysis software mentioned above!) Also included in this category is some version of **antivirus** software. At some point a **virus** will slip into your system, and if allowed to remain and spread, can inflict anything from annoying messages to complete destruction of your file system. A good antivirus program, with current updates, will detect and eliminate over 99 percent of infections, saving you countless hours of grief and frustration. Norton and McAfee are leading companies in this category as well. And if you have a high-speed internet connection, such as DSL or cable modem, then you definitely need to get a personal **firewall** package to defend your system against all the hackers out there. People who connect only by modem are usually at less of a risk, because they spend less time connected, and because their connection is slower. In many cases, the hackers just want to take over systems so that they can then use them to attack other sites anonymously (that is, they take over your system and then make it look like YOU are the bad guy!), and modem connections just aren't much use to them. A system with a high-speed connection that is usually on is a much juicier target, however, and my firewall alerts me several times each day that it has blocked attacks of various sorts. I am running Norton Internet Security, and while there may be better products out there, it is good enough, and I like its ease of configuration and use. Windows XP has a firewall built in, but you need to make sure that it is configured according to your needs.

In summary, software has been written to accomplish an incredible number of tasks. It is usually just a matter of finding it, installing it, and learning how to use it.

7

Upgrade an Old System?

A common question from people who bought a computer a few years ago is "Can't I just **upgrade** my old system rather than buying a whole new one?" The answer is not a simple yes or no, but we will look at some options.

Before you decide whether to upgrade or buy a complete new system, decide what it is that bothers you about your present system. If all you need is a faster modem, or more hard drive space, then an upgrade to your present system is a no-brainer. In fact, if you can upgrade it to fully satisfactory performance without spending more than $200 or so, then an upgrade may make more economic sense than a new system. Please note that if you are paying a service person to perform the upgrade, you are probably limited to a RAM upgrade or a new modem, because the labor cost will far outweigh the actual parts. If you can do the work yourself, or if you have a competent friend that you can call upon, then hard drive upgrades or installation of a CD-RW become doable. If you need (or would just like) more of an upgrade than this, then it is probably time to look for a new system. In any case, the time to upgrade is when you are really fed up with the limitations on your present one. As long as it does what you want in a satisfactory manner, then keep using it.

If you are considering an upgrade to your present system, then you should first consider its age. If it is more than three years old, then upgrading it to a useful level will probably cost more than buying a new one.

If your system is less than three years old, then the answer becomes more complex. The following list itemizes the common components that people upgrade. If you need to upgrade more than three of them, or if your total upgrade cost will exceed $200–$300, then you should probably put your money into a new system instead.

CPU/Motherboard

RAM

Hard Drive

Video card/monitor

Modem

The first upgrade to consider is a new CPU and/or motherboard. If your motherboard supports a faster CPU, then you may be tempted to just pop a new CPU in and go with it, but in most cases, a new motherboard and CPU is a better choice. This will get you the latest technology in terms of BIOS, external cache, and PCI and AGP slots, and will probably run twice as fast as your old board, even with the same CPU.

Motherboards are now available that include a sound card and video controller on the motherboard, which means that those upgrades are also included in the motherboard upgrade. Neither will be the best technology available, but should still be much better than what you are now using.

Note: Many name-brand manufacturers use proprietary case designs that cannot accept generic motherboards. Before attempting to upgrade a motherboard, make sure that a generic motherboard can fit your case. It is also difficult, and not usually worthwhile, to upgrade an older system that uses an AT power supply, to an **ATX** power supply. If you are contemplating an upgrade of this sort, you should plan to get a new system.

Rather than a motherboard upgrade, it is often simpler to buy a new **barebones** system consisting of case, power supply, motherboard, CPU, and possibly RAM. It is then quite simple to pull your drives from your old system and install them in the new one, keeping all your software and such just like you had it before.

Next, look at your **RAM**. Many systems sold 5 years ago had only

8–32 **MB** of RAM, and while that was adequate then, it is not adequate today. Windows 98 needs a minimum of 32 MB, while Windows XP needs 128 MB and works even better with 256 MB or more. The cost of RAM has declined to the point that adding 256 MB to your present system, or to a new motherboard, should cost less than $50 (or less than $120 for 256 MB of **RDRAM**, if that is what your system requires). However, make sure to purchase RAM that is compatible with your system.

Next consider your **hard drive**. If you still have only your original hard drive, then it may well be smaller than 4 GB, and is probably almost full. Hard drives are much cheaper today, and you could add a 40 GB drive for under $100. Another alternative, especially if you are planning to buy a new system in a few months and just want to extend the life of your current one a little longer is to install a Zip Drive, and then move it to your new system when you get it. With multiple 250 or even 750 MB cartridges, a Zip drive can give you a lot more room, plus it makes a very easy way to transfer everything to your new system. If your current system has a USB port, then get an external USB Zip drive, and you won't even need to open the case to install it, and moving it to the new system will take only seconds.

If your biggest frustration is how slow Windows is, then consider replacing your video card. A new AGP video card with 32 MB RAM can start below $40, and even some very fast ones are available for under $125. Virtually all new video cards are AGP, so if your system is old enough that it doesn't have an AGP slot, you will either have to look for an older card, perhaps on **eBay**, or perhaps it is time to upgrade your system. Just make sure that you have an available AGP slot before you buy an AGP card.

(A new video card combined with a RAM upgrade may make you think you have a new system, but make sure any components come with a 30-day money-back guarantee so that if they don't measure up, you can return them and put that money toward a new system.)

Do you use your modem a lot? If so, and it is slower than 28.8 kbps, upgrade to a **56K** version, and you will speed up your on-line sessions dramatically, regardless of the speed of your computer. Or, if you can get cable modem or DSL connections in your area, they will boost your surfing speed by a factor of 10–20 or more.

And of course, if you have an old 14" monitor with a dot pitch larger than 0.31 mm, then a new 17" or 19" monitor will give you room to enjoy all your new speed. And a new monitor will still be usable with a new system, so it should be considered separately from the general cost of upgrading the computer.

Do several of these upgrades sound necessary? If so, then it is probably time to buy a new computer rather than trying to upgrade. Otherwise, you could easily spend as much on your upgrades as a new system would cost, and you would still be stuck with some parts that would slow you down.

If your budget is strictly limited, but you still need the upgrade, and are not afraid to work inside your computer, I really recommend a new barebones system, which you can then continue to upgrade as your budget permits. However, by starting with a new case, motherboard, CPU, and RAM, you have a modern foundation on which to upgrade, rather than trying to put new components on your old system.

8

Buying a System

All right. You've read this far, talked to friends, and even shopped around some, but how do you decide what system you are actually going to get? First of all, don't expect to get the "best" deal. In my opinion, there is no such thing. Why not? Because the PC market is changing so fast, and there are so many factors that affect the value of a system, that in the end, determining what deal is best becomes a matter of opinion.

For example, if you found two identical systems, except that one had a one-year warranty and the other a two-year warranty, and the one with the two-year warranty cost $50 more, which one is the better deal? I can't say. It depends on how you feel about the value of warranties, and on the system itself. If neither system has any problems for the first two years, then the cheaper one is better, but you can't know that when you buy.

Since you will face dozens of decisions like this, how do you choose? I will now outline a strategy that should ensure that you get a good system at a competitive price, which is as much as you can really hope for.

First Step

Even if you intend to buy from a local dealer, go buy a copy of the latest *Computer Shopper* (at magazine racks and computer stores everywhere) and spend some time looking through it. Decide on a configuration that you would really like to have, but that is at least close to your budget (Table 1), and then start comparing different dealers.

Note: When comparing dealers, I strongly recommend that you NOT consider any mail-order companies that do not offer toll-free tech support for as long as you own the system, or that charge a **restocking fee** if you return the system for any reason. Mail-order companies that don't include toll-free tech support are essentially not including any cost for support, and you don't want to buy from anyone, local or mail-order, who doesn't plan and budget to support their products. Unless you feel competent to handle most of your own support needs, consider carefully the support policies of the company you buy from, even to the point of calling their tech support line to see how hard it is to get through.

TABLE 1. CHECKLIST

The system I want includes:

CPU	
RAM	
Floppy Drive(s)	
Zip Drive	
Hard Drive(s)	
Fax/modem	
CD-RW/DVD	
Sound card	
Monitor	
Video Card	
Case	

Other:________________________________

Use Table 1 as a checklist when reviewing an ad to make sure nothing was left out that matters to you. Also, if you want to include peripherals like a scanner, tape backup, or printer, you may get a better deal from a third party than from the computer dealer. At least know what peripherals should cost so when a dealer quotes a price, you know whether it's reasonable or not.

If you do not see a configuration that is close to what you want, then call their 800 number and ask for a system price on your configuration. Most dealers are willing to custom **configure** a system for you, for little more than the cost of the upgraded hardware itself, although it may take a few days longer to get the system shipped, since they won't have one pre-assembled according to your specifications.

The reason for the checklist (Table 1) showing what you want and can afford, is to help you compare similar systems. Some companies will not include a standard configuration in order to advertise a real eye-catching price. For example, some dealers advertise their systems without a monitor, so if you see a price that seems somewhat lower than any of their competitors, read the ad very carefully; there is almost certainly a corner cut somewhere. The experience of combing through the ads will also help when you talk to local dealers. If you know what things should cost, then you are less likely to be sold an overpriced system by a fast-talking salesman, or to find that what you thought was a complete system lacks some essential component.

Second Step

Make sure that your list has all the dealers on it that you are seriously considering. Include ONLY those companies that you would really consider buying from. Now sort through your list and pick out what appear to you to be the best three or four deals. These will not necessarily be the cheapest, but they should be competitive in price, and should offer good warranty and support.

Now call or visit each company and ask if the price is still the same for the configuration that you have used as your basis of comparison. Occasionally, you will find that prices have dropped, making the system an even better deal. Regardless, if the salesperson is courteous and helpful, write down their name and extension. Most of them get a commission on each sale they make, and it is not fair to them to take up their time getting information, and then call back later to buy, and give the deal to someone else. Of course, if they are not courteous, you probably won't be calling back there anyway.

These calls and visits should help you narrow down your field of choices to one or two, at which time, you are about ready to buy.

Note: Many people are reluctant to buy a computer from a mail-order firm, but there are tradeoffs to this choice. Mail-order companies will usually have a little lower prices than a local dealer, but if you have problems, it is much more satisfying to talk to someone face-to-face than over the phone. The quality of the help or repair may vary in any case, as there are a limited number of competent computer support people, and we can often only find out the hard way whether those in a particular store are competent. Many mail-order firms have problems with too many calls to their tech support lines, and reports of hours on hold, or voice mail messages that are never returned are far too common. This problem is especially acute for a month or two after Christmas, when millions of new users are struggling with their new systems.

If you have a reputable local dealer, or can find a suitable system at a local computer warehouse, then this is probably preferable to dealing with a mail-order firm. If you are not satisfied with your local choices, however, you will probably be able to get a good deal by mail-order. Reputable mail-order firms will give you a 30-day, money-back guarantee with no restocking fee. Since they don't want the system back, it will probably be just as represented.

Regardless of where you buy, however, you should pay by credit card. This way the credit card company protects you from fraud and theft. Another advantage is that many credit card companies will add up to a year of warranty coverage to your computer purchase, at no extra cost.

Third Step

Decide which system you want, and order it. If you purchase locally, you may be able to pick up your system the same day, unless you get a custom configuration.

Most mail-order vendors do not charge your credit card until they ship, but that may be as much as two weeks after you place your order, depending on their backlog and how quickly they get the system assembled. Most dealers "**burn in**" a new system for 48–72 hours, which means that after assembling it, they turn it on and let it run for that time. The reason for the burn-in is that if an electronic component is going to fail, it will usually do so quickly, so if no problems are apparent at the end of the burn-in, then it will probably be okay for years of use. Regardless of where you buy, you should burn it in yourself for the first week or so you have it. Just turn it on and let it run, and if problems develop, take it back at once!

If you buy by mail-order, then be aware that the most difficult time for a mail-order buyer is the interval between ordering and receiving

When Is a Good Time to Buy?

Many people want to know if there is a particular time of year that is better to buy computers. In general, the answer is no. There are always sales running at one store or another, and old models are being phased out as new ones come in. A possible exception is right after the Christmas shopping season, especially if dealers are left with a large inventory that they need to clear out, but even then, it is likely that by waiting two or three months prices on an equivalent system will be even lower.

In general, I recommend that you buy a new computer when the limitations of your old one become too annoying, or when there is a new application that you need that your old system just won't handle. In addition to the cost of the system itself, it is likely to cost you the better part of a week's work to transfer everything you need from the old system to the new one and to get it running smoothly, so plan your upgrade to avoid any foreseeable busy spells.

the new system. They think of all the things that could cause problems, and they see all sorts of deals that look like they might be better than the one that they got. The anxiety almost always ends when the new system arrives and is found to be in good shape.

Fourth Step

Set up your new system, turn it on, and use it a lot. If there are any problems, even minor annoyances, call tech support promptly and get them cleared up. Your first 30 days of ownership is a window when you can return a mail-order system if you really don't like it, so most dealers will go the extra mile during this period. If your system works well for the first 30 days, then it will probably work well for years.

Note: Many companies offer 30-day price protection, meaning that if the price of the system drops within 30 days of the time it is shipped, then they will credit you with the difference, but only if you ask.

Good luck, and happy computing!

PS—If you have Internet access, my e-mail address is:

gforeman@ix.netcom.com.

I love to hear from readers, and I value your input and suggestions.

Gordon Foreman
Los Alamos, NM

Appendix: Background and Explanation*

Cache: What Is It, and How Does It Work?

Note: While the principles described in this section apply just as much to the latest processors as to the earlier ones described, advances in CPUs, cache, RAM, etc., are such that using fully modern examples would be more confusing than helpful. Therefore, the explanations of cache that follow do not describe the latest technology. Also, it is of less interest now, since both L1 and L2 cache are always included in new systems, as integral parts of the CPU. Several years ago this was not the case, and the decision to pay to add an external cache to a system was not always obvious. At some point, this section will probably be dropped, unless reader feedback tells me it is still of interest.

Cache is used in two ways on a computer, but in both cases its purpose is to speed up the system. All caches operate by holding data in memory where it is more quickly accessible.

The first type of cache we will discuss is RAM cache, which comes in two forms; internal and external (also called L1 and **L2**, for level 1 and level 2). Internal cache is the 32KB found on the Pentium II/III/IV

**This section is included as a service to the curious reader who wants to better understand how a computer works. It is NOT necessary to understand the material in this Appendix in order to wisely purchase or use a computer. Indeed, most users don't know and don't care about such details.*

CPUs. Intel placed the cache there so that the CPU could hold the data that it used the most frequently where it would never need to wait for it to arrive. Without this internal cache, it would be pointless to make a clock-doubled chip that runs faster internally than externally, because it would have to wait after nearly every cycle for external data to arrive. This is why we never saw a clock-doubled 386; it didn't have an internal cache. However, 32KB, or 32,768 bytes, is not very large compared to the size of programs in use today, so the internal cache often has a miss. (When the cache has the data needed, it is called a "hit." When it doesn't, it is called a "miss.") When there is a miss, the CPU must wait while the data is retrieved from external memory, or even worse, from the hard drive.

On average, the internal cache has a hit about 90 percent of the time, but this is not good enough. Most **SDRAM** runs at 8 **ns** (nanoseconds, or billionths of a second), which roughly refers to how fast data can be retrieved. When a CPU is running externally at 100 MHz, it is completing an external cycle every 10 ns, so when it has to wait for data to arrive from RAM, it means a wait of at least four internal cycles for a 350 MHz or faster CPU. The reality may even be worse, because a few nanoseconds are lost checking to see if the internal cache has the data, then a few more are lost accessing the proper data in RAM, so this can easily extend to eight or twelve internal cycles. Thus, if you are using a PII and it must wait eight internal cycles every time the internal cache misses, then it is running at barely over half the speed it would if there were no misses. Does this seem excessive? Consider: It runs nine cycles of operation in which the data is available in the L1 cache, then waits eight cycles for data to arrive from RAM. Thus, it is waiting almost as much as it is working when the cache misses 10 percent of the time. However, it is running over five times as fast as it would without the L1 cache, since it complete ten operations in 19 internal cycles, rather than the two operations (almost) it could complete without cache.

Still, waiting half the time or more for data is unacceptable, so engineers figured out how to add external (or L2) cache to help speed things up. External cache was even added to a lot of 386 systems, since it isn't built into the CPU. External cache on a Pentium II system consists of high-speed synchronous RAM that is included in the CPU module itself, only an inch or two away from the CPU. (After all, there is no point in waiting for those electrons to travel farther than they have to, and the speed of light is about 1 foot per ns.) When the internal cache misses, then the CPU first checks to see if the data needed is in the external cache, before going to system RAM. A Celeron/A has 128K cache, a Pentium II has 512K, and a Xeon has either 512K, 1 MB, or 2 MB. External cache on a PII is accessed half the internal clock speed, though, so it always causes the CPU to wait one internal clock cycle. The Celeron and Xeon CPUs have a faster cache that is accessed at the internal clock speed, after a wait of a few clock cycles at the beginning of the access. It should be noted that the numbers that are used here are theoretical, and in reality, extra clock cycles are frequently required.

With external cache, let's re-examine the original scenario. The CPU works merrily along for nine cycles, and then finds that the data needed is not in the internal 32K cache. Now it goes to check the external cache. If it finds the data there, then it can proceed after a wait of only 1 cycle (or with no delay on the Celeron or Xeon). If it does not, then it still must wait eight internal cycles as it did before. However, since the external cache is much larger than the internal cache, it is much more likely to have the needed data. The combined cache hit rate for internal and external caches is on the order of 98 percent with an external cache of 128K and 99.5 percent with 512K.

Let's extend the work period to 200 operations and total up the number of cycles required to complete them. This assumes one operation completed per effective internal cycle, although Pentium II/III CPUs often handle more than one instruction per cycle.

Size of external cache	None	128K	512K
Operations/internal hit cycles	180/180	180/180	180/180
Operations/external hit cycles*	0	16/16	19/38
Operations/RAM access cycles	20/160	4/32	1/8
Total cycles req'd for 200 operations	340	228	226

**Assumes one internal clock cycle of delay while reading from the external cache for the 512K Pentium II cache, and no delay for the faster 128K Celeron/A cache.*

Thus, an external cache will speed up operations by 30–35 percent by reducing the clock cycles needed to perform 200 operations from 340 to 226–228, depending on the amount and speed of cache, so disabling the external cache is not a good idea. It is also worth noting that 128K of cache with no delay is equal to 512K with one cycle of delay. It is also interesting that our very idealized numbers indicate performance very close to what is actually found in a variety of benchmarks.

The above computation assumes that the CPU only needs to get data from the cache, but in reality it also needs to save data. Early caches provided only for reading data, and the system had to wait for the CPU to write (save) data to RAM, just as if no cache were present. Since writing data is nearly as slow as reading it, this caused significant delays. Modern caches are "write-back" meaning that the CPU writes the data to the cache and then proceeds, while the system then transfers this data on back to the RAM without input from the CPU. Write-back caches are thus faster than the older "write-through" caches that required the CPU to write directly back to system RAM.

An even more recent innovation is pipelined burst cache. In older L2 cache, the CPU had to pause frequently to verify what data/program code is in the cache, but a pipelined burst cache sends long streams of data to and from the CPU. All CPUs since the Pentium II incorporate both write-back and pipeline technology, as well as other tweaks and tricks to speed data on its way.

The third type of cache is a disk cache. Occasionally, the data the CPU needs is not available in RAM, and so it must copied from the hard drive. The hard drive is much slower than RAM, and the CPU may well wait for several *million* internal cycles for this data to arrive. To minimize such waits, a disk cache is used, which is RAM that holds the data from the hard drive that is stored sequentially after the data just requested, in the expectation that this is likely to be the data that the CPU will request next. If it is right, then the CPU can proceed after only 20–30 cycles, rather than 1,000,000 or more. Disk caches can either use some of the system RAM to store disk data (software cache), or can use RAM built into the hard drive or its **controller** (hardware cache). Either way, every system should have some sort of disk cache, but this need not involve extra expense. Disk caching is built into all current versions of Windows.

A related technology is the reverse of disk cache, called **virtual memory**. Because sometimes the computer needs more RAM than is available, especially when several applications are open at once, virtual memory allows the computer to use hard drive storage to mimic RAM. Of course, it may be a million times slower, but the software is designed to place programs and data in virtual memory that are accessed only rarely, or that have not been accessed recently. For example, suppose you have Word running in the background, but have not accessed it for several minutes while you were surfing the Internet. Then when you try to bring Word back up, it takes a few seconds to respond. In a case like this, it is very likely that the computer had shifted Word to virtual memory, and the delay was the time that it took to move something else to virtual memory and put Word back in RAM or active memory. If such delays are common on your system, then adding more RAM may reduce or eliminate this problem.

Hard Disks and RAM: How Does a Computer Work?

Since the size of the **hard drive** and the amount of **RAM** in a computer are both measured in **MB** (megabytes) or **GB** (gigabytes), many people are confused about what the difference is, and what role each plays on a PC.

Let me create a brief analogy that may help. If you consider your computer to be like your office at work, then the hard disk would be like your bookshelves and file cabinets. It is the place that you store information that you are not working on at the moment. Thus, if you had only a two-drawer file cabinet or one bookshelf, you might quickly find yourself without any place to store new information. You can add more file cabinets or shelves, however, just like you can add another hard drive, or replace your old one with a larger one. Thus, a common synonym for available hard drive space is storage.

RAM, on the other hand, is your active workspace, much like your desk. If you had only a small desk, say the size of a TV tray, it would be very difficult to work, because you wouldn't have enough room. It would be impossible to work on more than one task at a time. However, if you replaced your small desk with a large executive version, or added a large work table, then you would have ample room to spread things out. One important difference, however, is that RAM holds information only as long as the computer is turned on. When the computer is turned off, everything in RAM disappears. This is like having a desk where everything magically disappears when you turn out the light, so it is very important to save your work before turning off a computer. A common synonym for RAM is memory.

The upside of this is that whenever you open a file or program from your hard drive into RAM, you actually *copy* the file into RAM: The original remains on the hard drive. Thus, when the computer shuts down (or worse, when it locks up or crashes), everything that has not been saved to the hard drive is gone, and cannot be retrieved later, while everything that was saved earlier should be on your hard drive. Some programs feature an "auto-save" option that will automatically save your work in progress every few minutes, but it is better not to depend on them. Save files shortly after you start working on them, and save them frequently as you continue to work on them.

Hard Drive Compression: What Is It?

Disk compression is an option that allows you to store more data on your hard drive. It is often referred to simply as compression. This term is misleading, because the disk is not changed in any way at all. Instead, the data on the disk is manipulated to store it in a smaller space, allowing more data to fit on the same size of drive, so it really should be called data compression.

Data is compressed by removing redundant information. For example, suppose we had a file that said "Mary had a little lamb. Mary had a little lamb. Mary had a little lamb. Mary had a little lamb. Mary had a little lamb." This could be replaced with "Mary had a little lamb. (Repeat 5 times)" so instead of 120 characters (counting spaces) it would have only 40 characters. Real life is more complex, but most text files have enough redundancy that they can be reduced by 30–50 percent or more in this manner. Compression software compresses and decompresses files as they are called for, usually without a noticeable delay. In fact, when loading data from a CD-ROM or the Internet, compressed files often load faster, because a compressed file comes from the CD-ROM or modem faster than the uncompressed file, and the CPU can perform decompression of the file almost instantly. Thus, while drive compression is not common, given how large hard drives have grown, file compression is becoming almost the rule on the Internet. **JPEG**, **MPEG**, streaming video, and many other file formats use compression.

The only downside to disk compression is that the compression-decompression process can scramble an entire file, or even a whole disk, if a glitch occurs in the middle. I recommend that you use disk compression only if the loss of your data would not be a disaster, AND if you are seriously hurting for storage space. Also be aware that many games already store most of their files, especially graphics, in compressed form, so compressing your drive will not help you with them.

Which Operating System Should I Use?

With the appearance of **Windows XP**, many people are considering whether they should stick with Windows 95/98/ME or not. Of course, most new computers will come with Windows XP Home as the default (unless you are buying a work system, in which case it will come with XP Professional), and unless you have specific reasons for wanting an earlier version of Windows, XP is almost certainly the best choice, since it is far more stable and less subject to crashes than Windows 98/ME. Windows XP Home is the first home use operating system built on the same computer code as Windows 2000, and it incorporates many features that make it more stable. However, I would only recommend upgrading an older system to XP if you are having serious problems. In fact, rather than upgrade an older system, you should back up all of your data and reformat your hard drive, or simply install a new hard drive, and then do a clean install of Windows XP, since a clean install is far less likely to have problems than an upgrade from an earlier version. It will take more time and effort, but this really is one of those "pay me now or pay me later" situations.

DOS/Windows: Unless you are running old hardware that will not support a newer operating system, this is not your best bet. On the other hand, there are old legacy applications that will not run under any other operating system, and if you need to run one of these, you may have no choice. However, none of the programs written in the last few years will work on such an old system, so your upgrade options are limited. Typically, if people need DOS/Windows 3.x, then they keep an older system for that purpose, but get a new system to run current software.

Windows NT 4.0/Windows 2000: NT 4.0 has been available since September 1996, and is still in widespread use, but it is being replaced by Windows 2000 and/or Windows XP Professional. **Win2K** includes all the features that made NT a popular operating system in the business world, and adds to it numerous features that make it more stable and easier to configure. Windows XP adds even more new features, but is really a much more incremental upgrade from Windows 2000. Microsoft has said that as of June 30, 2003, they will stop supporting Windows NT.

Win2K requires an absolute minimum of 64 MB of RAM, and really needs 128 MB or more. XP is even more demanding, needing at least 128 MB, and preferably more. Microsoft has published a Hardware Compatibility List for NT/2K/XP, and if you want to run either one, every single component in the computer must be on the list, or it almost certainly won't work. It also needs as fast a CPU as you can afford.

The great strengths of Win2K/XP include its security and stability, meaning that it is difficult to hack into (or at least it can be configured to be so—it doesn't tend to come set up that way on new systems, however), and a program that crashes will rarely bother the rest of the system. However, Microsoft's e-mail program, Outlook/Outlook Express, is vulnerable to a huge number of **viruses**, **worms**, and **trojan horses**, most of which specifically target Outlook, and are not a threat to any other e-mail program. Likewise, Microsoft's Internet Information Server, or IIS, which is the web server built into Windows 2000 Server has been reported to have numerous security vulnerabilities, each of which has a patch, but if you are running IIS, you need to be very diligent about applying these patches, or hackers may have easy access to your system.

If you are buying a new system for a business environment, then Win2K or Windows XP Professional is highly recommended, although I would only upgrade an older system running Windows NT if that system were having problems. The time to move to XP is when you buy a new system. "If it ain't broke, don't fix it." For the home environment, however, I would stick with Windows XP Home.

Windows 98/ME: If you are running Windows 98 or Windows ME on an existing system, and you are not having too many problems, then keep using it. However, with a new system I would definitely recommend using Windows XP.

Windows 95: This was Microsoft's standard home and small business operating system for nearly three years, and is still widely used. Some of its advantages over DOS/Windows 3.x include long files names (up to 255 characters), faster operation with true 32-bit software, much better memory handling, excellent operation of DOS games, a much more intuitive interface, and finally, it was the first operating system for PCs to support **PNP** (plug and play). However, all versions of Windows that are more recent include compelling advantages, so I really don't recommend Windows 95.

Linux: This is a freeware operating system similar to Unix that has been around since 1991, and that is becoming widely popular. Although no specific company owns it, there are several companies that have developed distributions of Linux and who will sell you a CD (or set of CDs) with all the installation files needed to set it up and run it. A distribution typically includes much more than just the operating system, and usually includes software to help users install and configure it. Given that most people in the PC environment are not experienced with Linux, this is a smart move. There are several distributions that are gaining widespread use in the United States, including Red Hat, Caldera, Mandrake, and Lindows. Support can be purchased from any of these companies, but is typically provided by thousands of dedicated users over the Internet, which is actually where most of its popularity resides.

Lindows in particular is pushing hard to develop market share by offering a "click and run" service whereby people who are willing to pay $129 or so per year have access to well over a thousand applications that they can download, install, and run at no further cost. Programs thus available include office suites, photo editing software, internet browsers, and virtually everything else you might want, except for games. There are certainly games available, but only a few of the popular Windows-based games have yet been ported over to Linux. As demand grows, however, this may change.

The Apache web server, which runs under Linux, is the most popular web server software in use, and if you are considering setting up a web server, or want to learn how to set one up, you will probably want to use either Linux, or run IIS (Internet Information Server) under Windows 2K/XP. Linux has a reputation for being much more stable than Windows, and for needing much less in the way of hardware. In many instances, older systems that are otherwise being phased out can serve very nicely as Linux web servers.

For a home or small office system, Linux has progressed to the point where it is a viable option, as long as games are not high on your list of needs. Certainly you can do nearly anything else that you need to do on a Linux system, and typically at a much lower cost. The only serious caveat here is that if you know Windows but don't know Linux, then the learning curve will be fairly steep for the first few weeks while moving over. On the other hand, if I were trying to set up a business with 20 or more users, I would seriously consider running Linux rather than Windows, simply because the cost of the operating system and other software would be $500–$1000 per user less than with Windows, depending on what software was installed.

I currently have a system running Mandrake Linux 9.0, and I like it very well, although I still do most of my work in Windows, simply because that is where I am most comfortable. On the other hand, I really like the idea of having more control of my system, and not having to deal with product activation codes and hassles like that. Having purchased CDs with Mandrake Linux on them, I am free to install it on as many systems as I want to, without ever infringing on anyone's copyright.

What Does the Future Hold?

Other than a few obvious trends, I don't know. It seems apparent that computers will continue to become more powerful and less expensive, but specific features are hard to predict. However, I will describe a feature that I would like to see, and that I have never seen described anywhere else. I call it the I-ball.

I have read that pilots of some attack helicopters have an aiming mechanism called "look and shoot." It consists of one or more tiny, low power, infrared lasers that constantly track the position of the pilots eyeballs, such that all he has to do is look at a target and squeeze the trigger. The aiming of the gun is automatically slaved to his eyeballs so that where ever he looks is where the bullets go.

I would like a similar unit that sits on top of my monitor and tracks my eyes, such that where ever I look on the monitor and click a control key, the cursor will move there and be ready for action. I would then be able to select with a single click, open with a double click, or click and drag, using my eyes to move icons and such around the screen.

This wearable computer was being demonstrated at a trade show. The object in front of my right eye is a tiny video screen. Note also the microphone, the video camera on the left side of my head, and the keyboard on my left arm. My right hand is on the mouse control. Not the sort of computer most of us need for surfing the web or word processing, but the cool factor is very high. It was being promoted as a tool for maintenance workers, airline mechanics, etc., where they could call up maintenance manuals and such while leaving their hands free, and where they could also show staff back in the control room what the problem was through their video camera.

This would enable me to dispense completely with the mouse, and the need to move my hands away from the keyboard. This would be an especially powerful option for handicapped people who lack hand mobility, especially if it were coordinated with voice recognition. It would then be possible to easily control a computer without any input but eyes and voice. For people who lack adequate voice control, it should even be possible to learn special eye-blink patterns that would allow them to control the computer with nothing but their eyes.

For the rest of us it would simply be the most intuitive interface yet for moving around and doing things, as well as a real boon for people suffering from carpal tunnel syndrome or tendonitis.

I have no doubt that such a unit would be expensive to develop, but they should be fairly inexpensive to build, especially in large volume, and as the price dropped below $100 or so, demand would be tremendous.

Such a unit could also serve a secondary function of performing an iris scan to identify the user of the computer, such that only authorized users would be able to log onto or operate the system. There are a number of **biometric** identity verification devices on the market, but combining these two functions would make them very popular in environments where system security is essential.

It would also be a great enhancement for many mobile or portable computers. The picture on the previous page shows the author wearing a computer that was being demonstrated at a trade show. It had a small lever similar to a joystick that served as a mouse, but the ability to control the cursor with my eye would have been a huge improvement.

Other Useful PC Reference Books

PC Buyer's Handbook has a very narrow focus. If you are interested in the broader topic of how computers work, then there are a number of books on the market that can tell you all you want to know, and more. Those I mention here I consider quite good, but there are a number of others that are probably as good. Go to a bookstore that carries a good selection of computer books, and spend a while browsing around.

If you really don't know much about computers, and want basic explanations written at about a *Reader's Digest* level, then either of the following books should answer most of your questions.

PCs for Dummies from IDG.

If you want more in-depth information about every little detail of how PCs work, then either of the following may give you what you want.

The Hardware Bible by Winn L. Rosch.
Inside the PC, by Peter Norton.

Finally, if you are looking for more information about upgrading or repairing PCs, then either of the following should help you out.

Upgrading PCs for Dummies from IDG.
The Complete PC Upgrade and Maintenance Guide by Mark Minasi.

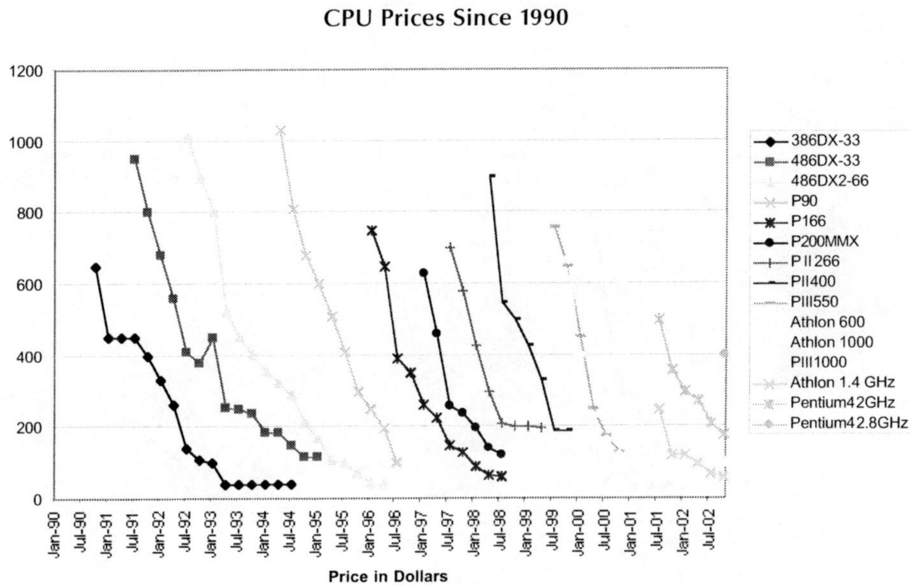

Figure A-1

The CPU prices shown above are as accurate as I could determine from the *Computer Shopper* or on the Internet. They are the lowest prices I could find, not an average price. In some cases, when I could not find a price for a CPU by itself, I estimated the cost by comparing systems that were identically configured except for the CPU. Regardless of exact costs, the trends are obvious.

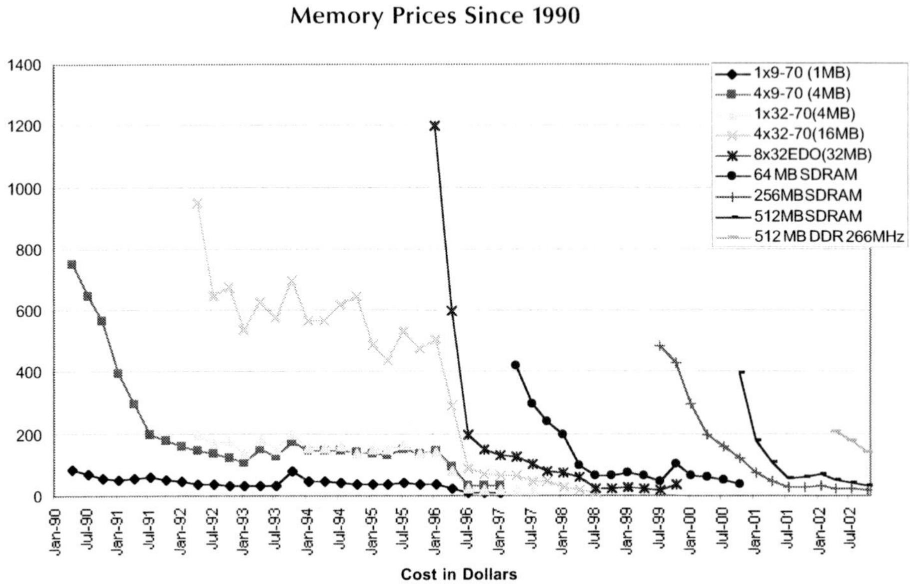

Figure A-2

The price per MB for SIMMs was nearly flat until the end of 1995, but since that time prices have declined from around $40 per MB to as little as $0.10 per MB. This is one of the largest causes of the drop in computer prices during this time.

With the advent of the Pentium II and later CPUs, the market has shifted from 72-pin SIMMs to the 168-pin DIMMs. The companies that make RAM have invested billions of dollars in plants that make larger DIMMs (64–512 MB) and it seems unlikely that RAM prices will ever go back up significantly, although blips may occur due to temporary circumstances.

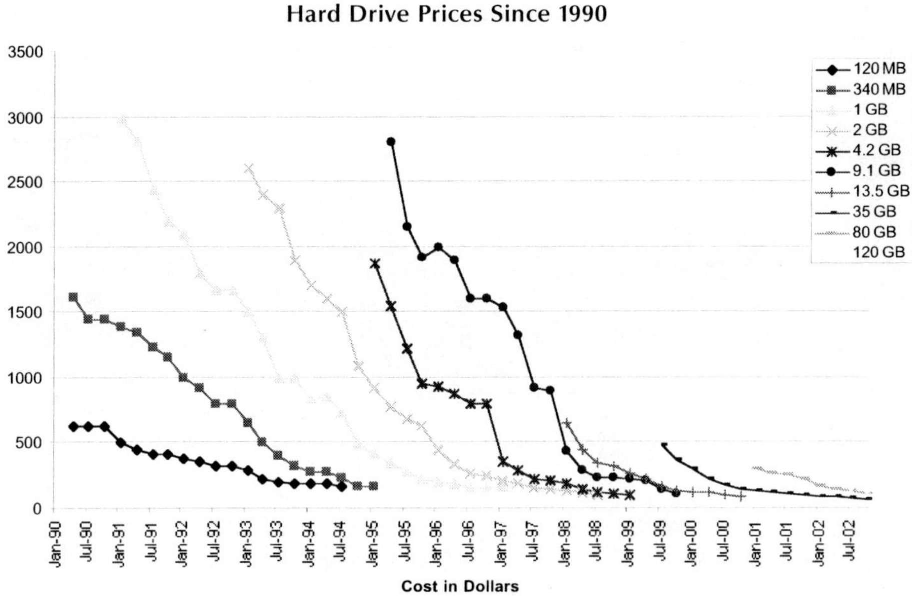

Figure A-3

As is evident from this chart, hard drive prices have plummeted, and there is no evidence that the trend is about to stop. Just ten years ago, most home systems came with hard drives in the 80–200 MB range; now most come with 20–80 GB or more. It appears that the price floor for every hard drive is around $120. When a drive's price declines to this level, manufacturers discontinue it shortly thereafter, and the market moves to the next larger size. Thus, 40 GB drives are now close out items, and the 80 GB drives will be there sometime next year.

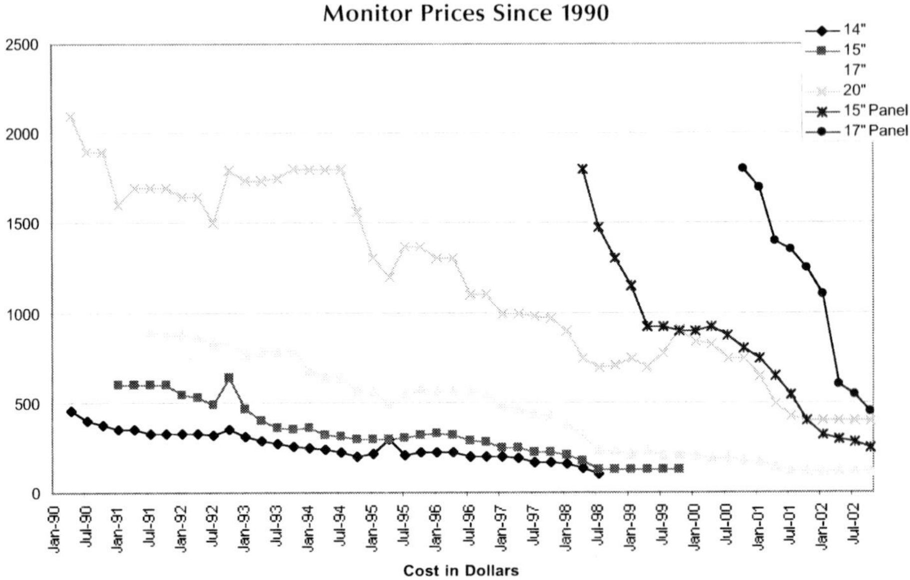

Figure A-4

Although this graph shows gradual declines in monitor prices over the last few years (at least compared to other computer components), it does not take into account the rapidly increasing capabilities of monitors during that period. Virtually all monitors sold today support 1024 × 768 resolution noninterlaced, and nearly all have a dot pitch of 0.31 mm or less. Monitors with a larger dot pitch are still sold in some places, but they are usually older units that are being cleared from stock. 17" monitors are now widely available for under $150, which puts them within reach of many home users. 21" monitors are dropping even faster, but most home users have neither the need nor the space for a 21" monitor. Actually, although I didn't include them in the chart, 19" monitors have become very popular, with prices typically about $100 higher than 17" monitors.

Flat-panel displays, like those used on portable systems, but designed for use with desktop computers, are still more expensive than CRTs, but are now priced where many home users can afford them. I have seen prices as low as $400 for a 15" screen, and $650 for a 17" screen. In the long run, though, flat panel monitors should largely replace the CRT monitors that we are accustomed to.

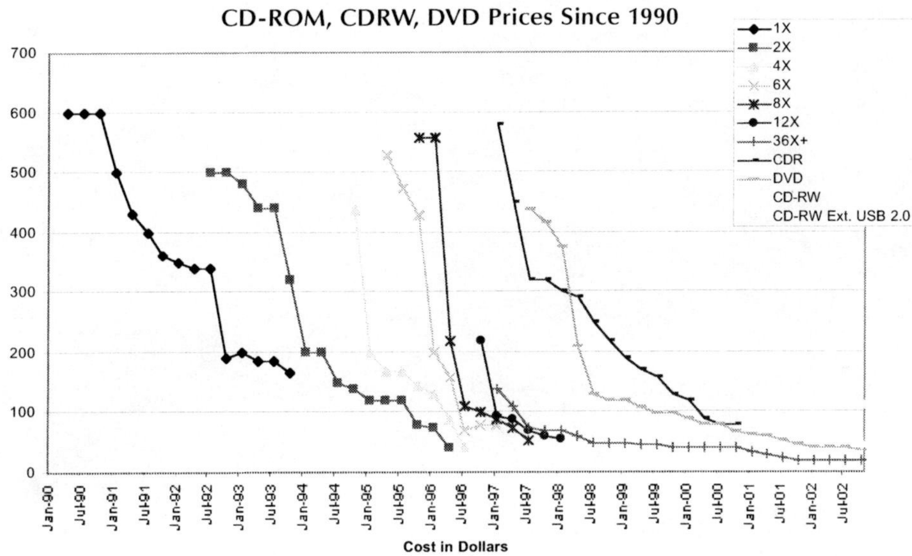

Figure A-5

CD-ROM prices have dropped dramatically, and on all but the cheapest systems, are being replaced by either CD-RW (read-write) or DVD-ROM drives, or both. A combination drive that serves as both a CD-RW and DVD is also available, and is a very popular choice on new systems.

Glossary of Terms and Abbreviations

10/100 network card A network card that will support either 10 megabits per second or 100 megabits per second of data transfer. The lower speed continues to be supported because so many other networking components were designed to operate at this speed.

16.7 million colors *see* 24-bit color.

1.2V 1.2 volts. A power-saving, heat-reducing voltage now in wide use. Until 1993, nearly all CPUs operated at 5 volts, but the need for portables that run longer on batteries and for CPUs that incorporate more but smaller elements means that virtually all CPUs now on the market use from 0.9 to 1.45 volts.

24-bit color Also known as true-color. Color on a computer monitor is generated by mixing various intensities of red, green, and blue. On a 24-bit color display, 8 bits are assigned to each of these three colors for each pixel, allowing each color to have 256 (2^8) degrees of intensity, from 0 to 100 percent. When you multiply 256 possible intensities of red times 256 possible intensities of green times 256 possible intensities of blue, you get a total of 16.7 million different colors that can be displayed on each pixel of the screen. The human eye cannot distinguish this many different shades, so it is described as true-color; that is, the human eye cannot see any colors in the image that vary from the original.

32-bit Computer hardware or operating system that handles data in 32-bit chunks.

386 A shortened way of referring to the Intel 80386 CPU, as well as compatible CPUs made by other companies. No longer being built for desktop systems, although I hear that millions of them are used as embedded controllers in cars and other places.

486 A shortened way of referring to the Intel 80486 CPU, as well as compatible CPUs made by other companies.

56K The current high end of modems. If it does not also say V.90, then it may only conform to either the X2 or 56K Flex standards, which were only compatible at speeds of 33.6 and slower. V.90 is the unification standard that every 56K modem should support. V.92 includes the latest updates to the standard.

6X Six-speed something, usually CD-ROMs. When CD-ROMs first came out, they turned at the same speed as music CDs, but while that is adequate for flawless music reproduction, it provides a very slow data transfer. So they started speeding up CD-ROM drives, first to 2X, then to 3X, and so on, until today most run at a maximum speed of 12 to 56 times the speed of a music CD player. Of course, the actual speed depends on the part of the disk that is being accessed, and data retrieval speeds are not 12 to 56 times faster except under very special conditions.

80×86 The whole series of CPUs, from the 8086 through the Pentium IV, that have a backward compatible design.

AC adapters Portable computers don't usually have a power supply built in, so an AC adapter supplies DC current for the system to operate and/or recharge.

accelerated Refers to video cards that include an accelerator chip that speeds up Windows. May also be used to refer to any component that uses a special chip or embedded code to run faster than earlier versions.

active matrix The best, brightest, and most expensive color screen for a portable system. Also called TFT or TFTN.

ADSL Asynchronous Digital Subscriber Line. This is a high-speed digital phone line that supports megabit connection speeds, and can be used for voice, fax, and Internet at the same time. It is only available within about three miles of the telephone company switching station, and only where phone companies have upgraded their equipment to support it. Same as DSL.

AGP Accelerated Graphics Port. A new video interface design from Intel that greatly speeds up video displays, without adding to the traffic on the PCI bus. Nearly all now run at 4X or 8X, i.e., four or eight times faster than the original AGP slot.

AMD Advanced Micro Devices. This company makes the Athlon and Duron CPUs that compete with those made by Intel.

antivirus Refers to programs such as Norton Antivirus or McAfee VirusScan that detect and protect against computer viruses. See *virus* for more details.

ATA Same thing as EIDE. Ultra ATA supports drives larger than 8.4 GB.

AT Bus *see* ISA Bus.

ATAPI AT Application Programming Interface. Another name for EIDE.

Athlon The high-end CPU from AMD that is the chief competitor to the Intel Pentium IV.

ATX A new motherboard design from Intel that minimizes problems with long cards hitting the CPU or SIMMs. Also defines a new power supply standard that can start the system remotely from a modem or network signal, or at a preset time. Not compatible with old case designs, however.

average seek time Average time that it takes for a hard drive or CD-ROM to begin reading the data requested, measured from the time the request was made. This number is given in milliseconds (ms) or thousandths of a second.

bandwidth A measure of how rapidly data can be transferred. The wider the bandwidth, the more rapidly the data moves. A DSL or cable modem has much higher bandwidth than a modem.

benchmark A program that measures the speed of a CPU, video card, hard drive, etc.

beta The last version of a software program before it is marketed. Typically beta versions still have diagnostic code included in them, and they are likely to have more bugs and problems than the final version, since the beta version is sent out to users so that they can find problems.

biometric Having to do with unique individual body characteristics, such as fingerprints, handprints, voiceprints, retinal patterns, or the iris. Passwords are easily forgotten, and can also be shared or stolen, whereas biometric features are unique to each of us, and don't require that we memorize anything. As such, many experts predict that computer security will mostly move to biometric measures over the next few years.

BIOS Basic Input/Output System. The BIOS is the part of the system that determines what to do with each electronic signal that goes through the system. Until a BIOS was developed that exactly replicated the IBM BIOS for every possible command, true "IBM Compatible" systems were not possible.

bit The smallest possible piece of computer data, it is either a 0 or 1. Eight bits make a byte, which equals one letter.

bleeding edge A pun on the term "leading edge." Many PC users who buy the latest technology find themselves uncovering and struggling with previously unidentified problems or bugs. Thus, the leading edge became the bleeding edge.

bootleg To make illegal copies of software.

boot up To start up a computer.

bps Bits per second. Usually refers to fax/modems or CD-ROMs. *See also* kbps.

BSB Back side bus. The connection between the CPU and the PCI slots and cards. *See also* **FSB**.

bundle The practice of putting together a bunch of options, including hardware and software, for an advertised price. Usually, dealers are unwilling to give significant discounts for "unbundling" portions that you don't want/need.

burn in The process of turning on a computer and letting it run for a day or more after it is fully assembled. If an electronic part is going to fail, the probability is high that it will fail in the first few hours of operation, so burning in a system allows the dealer to replace any such parts before shipping the system to a customer.

burning CDs To burn a CD is to record data on one in a CD-RW drive. Generally, this refers only to the CDR disks that cannot be overwritten, but it is sometimes used to describe writing data to a rewriteable disk as well.

bus The type of connection through which cards communicate with the CPU and the rest of the motherboard. The main types are ISA and PCI local bus. The AGP slot also falls into this category, although it is more specialized than the others.

byte A single character (letter, number, space, etc.) in computer code. It is composed of 8 bits. Note that the standard for abbreviating byte is to use a capital "B," whereas bit is abbreviated with a lowercase "b."

cable modem This is not actually a modem, but a network interface that allows users to access the Internet using the same cable through which they receive cable TV. Where available, it is a much faster choice than a regular modem.

cache High-speed RAM that speeds up data access for the CPU. Internal (L1) cache refers to the cache that is built into the CPUs, while external (L2) cache consists of SRAM chips that sit adjacent to the CPU. The L2 cache is built into the CPU module on the Pentium II/III/IV CPUs. See the Appendix if you want a more detailed explanation.

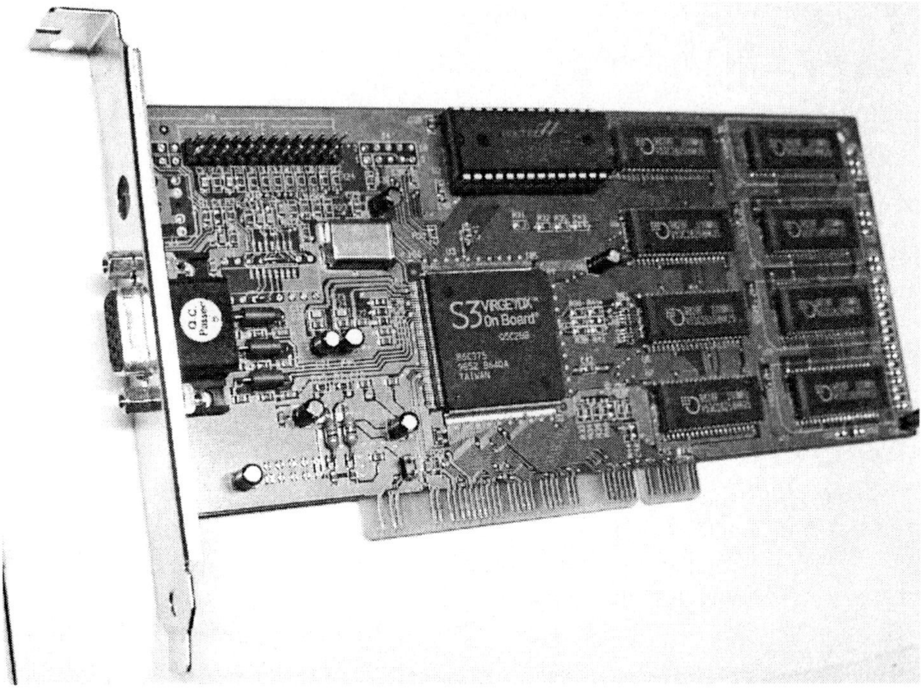

This is a PCI video card. Note the video port on the back, and the PCI connectors or contacts on the bottom.

CAD Computer-Aided Design. This does for engineering drawing and design what the word processor does for writing.

card The printed circuit boards that are added to a computer to add features or capabilities. For example, sound cards, video cards, serial cards, SCSI cards, etc.

case The outside part of the computer; the part you see. Cases come in several varieties, including Baby AT, mini, mid, and full tower, and mini desktop.

CAT-5 This refers to standard network hardware, cables, plugs, etc., that can support data transfer speeds up to 100 Mbps.

CDR/CD-RW CD-ROM Recordable or Rewriteable. These are CD-ROM drives that allow the user to record CDs as well as play them. It does require a special CD disk, as regular CDs cannot be written to.

CD-ROM Compact Disk-Read Only Memory. Compact disks like those used for music, but that instead store data. A CD-ROM can hold up to 680 MB.

Celeron This is the low end of the Pentium III/IV line. Intel introduced the Celeron in an effort to drive the market away from the Pentium clone CPUs made by AMD and Cyrix. Although they are the low end of Intel's line, they are actually only a few percent slower than P4 systems with the same clock speed. Unless you need the fastest system available, Celeron systems are a very cost-effective choice.

Centronics *see* Parallel.

communication Usually refers to modems or networks, or the hardware or software necessary to run them.

compatible Refers to hardware or software that is not made by the company that established the generally accepted standard, but that will work with it. Originally used to refer to non–IBM PCs that would nonetheless run all software written for the IBM PC family. Examples common today include CPUs not made by Intel, and sound cards not made by SoundBlaster.

configure To configure means to define what components are used to build a system. Thus, a standard configuration is one that the dealer puts together based on his judgment, while a custom configuration is one where the buyer specifies the components. Configure is also used in a setup sense, as where people have to configure the jumpers, switches, and other settings on a card so that it will work with the rest of the system.

controller Usually a card, but sometimes a chip, that controls something else. Most commonly refers to a controller for hard drives, floppy drives, CD-ROM, etc. Also used to describe the type of controller, as IDE, SCSI, etc.

This is an Athlon CPU typical of those used in many systems today.

CPU Central Processing Unit. The brain of the computer, such as the Pentium IV. Sometimes used to refer to the case and everything in it.

crash When it refers to a program, it means that a glitch has caused it to quit working, and that the program, and possibly the computer, will have to be restarted. When it refers to a hard drive or other hardware, it means that it has suffered a physical or mechanical malfunction and may have to be replaced.

CRT Cathode Ray Tube. This is the monitor that looks like a TV. It is actually shooting an electron beam from the back of the tube to the glass in front, where it hits various phosphors that then glow to create the image. If speakers are placed too close to the sides of the monitor, the image can be distorted. *Note:* There is no real danger (to people) to working inside the case of a computer, but you should NEVER remove the case on a CRT unless you are a trained technician. The tube can hold a high-voltage charge for days after it is turned off, and if you touch the wrong place, it will zap you, possibly even lethally.

cursor The point on the screen where you can change things. It may be a blinking line, or an arrow, or a number of other things. The cursor keys are the ones with arrows that allow you to move the cursor around. In Windows, the mouse moves the cursor as well. (Not to be confused with curser, which is what most of us are when a program crashes and we lose the work we have been doing.).

data transfer rate The measure of how fast data is transferred from a hard drive or CD-ROM to RAM or to another drive.

database A program that is used to track large amounts of data, like customer records, or a phone book. Even a Christmas card list or a recipe program would qualify as a database.

DDR Double Data Rate. This refers to a design for RAM that allows faster access while using the cheaper **SDRAM** modules. The alternative is to go to **RDRAM**, which is much more expensive, but not a lot faster in practice.

desktop publishing Abbreviated DTP. This is the process of preparing text, graphics, headers, etc., for publication in a newsletter, etc.

digital camera A digital camera looks very much like a normal camera, but rather than saving a picture on film, it saves it as an electronic image that can then be transferred to a computer and viewed on screen. Many digital cameras have a small **LCD** screen on the back of the camera that lets you preview pictures as soon as they are taken, with the option to erase them at once if you don't like what you took.

DIMM Dual In-line Memory Module. Synchronous DRAM (SDRAM) comes in DIMMs, and most current Pentium motherboards support them, as well as SIMMs. Current motherboards usually support only DIMMs.

DIP switches Dual In-line Package switches. Usually a small plastic module (mounted on a card or motherboard) that has several small on/off switches that can be used to set different modes of operation.

disk compression The process of removing redundant information from data and programs stored on disk so that more space is available. The Windows 95 Plus Pack included compression software, as do current versions of Windows, but with current hard drive capacities, it is rarely needed.

DMA Channel Direct memory access channel. PCs have 8 DMA channels, and many peripherals such as sound cards must have one of them dedicated for their use.

docking station Portable computers can plug into a docking station and essentially become a desktop system, with connections to a network, regular keyboard and mouse, a full-size monitor, external Jaz, Zip, CD-ROM drives, etc.

dot matrix One of the first common types of printers. Dot matrix printers force small pins out to hit a ribbon, transferring ink to the paper, as the print head moves across. Older printers were mostly 9-pin, while most later ones are 24-pin, and provide much better print quality. However, unless you need to print multi-part forms, a dot-matrix printer is probably not your best choice today.

dot pitch Refers to the size in millimeters (mm) of each dot or pixel on a monitor. Good monitors have a dot-pitch of 0.28 mm or less. If the dot-pitch is larger than 0.31 mm, then the screen will be unduly fuzzy.

download The process of receiving a file from a website. Sending a file to a website is an upload. If it is sent as an e-mail attachment, then it is simply called an attachment.

dpi Dots per inch. Almost always refers to the resolution on a printer. The larger the number, the clearer the text, in theory. In reality, other factors such as the size of each dot and the darkness of the ink also affect print quality. Most laser or inkjet printers have a resolution of 300, 600, or more dpi.

DRAM *see* RAM.

DSL Digital Subscriber Line. *See also* ADSL.

dual scan passive matrix The second-best type of color screen for portable computers after active matrix. Also called DSTN. *Note:* If privacy while working on your portable system is a real concern, then you may prefer a dual scan screen because the image is very difficult to see unless you are directly in front of it. Snoopers will not be able to see it clearly unless they look right over your shoulder. Not usually available on new systems today.

Duron A lower-end version of the Athlon CPU that AMD developed to compete with the Celeron CPU from Intel.

DVD Digital video disc. An enhanced CD-ROM drive that can read discs holding up to several GB. First generation DVD drives should be avoided, as there were some compatibility issues with some disks. However, the newer DVD drives can read both CD-ROM and DVD disks, and with appropriate connections, can allow you to view DVD movies, either on your monitor or on a TV.

eBay An auction site that is one of the most successful businesses based on the Internet. You can find almost anything here, including computers.

EIDE Enhanced IDE. An extension of the IDE standard to allow a single controller to handle up to four (as opposed to two) hard drives, each of which can be up to 8.4 GB (as opposed to 528 MB under IDE). A further upgrade in Pentium II/III/IV systems allows drives up to 130 GB and modern motherboards support drives that can be millions of times larger than that.

e-mail Electronic mail. For people who become accustomed to using on-line services, e-mail is usually much preferred to paper mail, or snail mail, as it is often called. E-mail arrives almost instantaneously, regardless of the distance between sender and recipient, and is free, even to foreign countries, except for a monthly access fee for Internet service.

Energy Star A standard for energy efficiency and conservation in computers and peripherals.

Enhanced IDE *see* EIDE.

ergonomic Any design that considers human needs and is less likely to cause injury or disability as a result of prolonged use. You should be aware that not everybody finds every ergonomic design suitable. Often used as a buzzword by sales people.

FAT-32 The 32-bit File Allocation Table incorporated into Windows 98 and ME and the last version of Windows 95, FAT-32 provides for much more efficient storage of data on large hard drives, and allows partitions up to several hundred GB. However, it is not readable by either earlier versions of Windows 95 or by Windows NT, although Windows 2000 and Windows XP can read it.

fax Short for facsimile. Allows transmission of pages of text and graphics via phone line to other fax machines.

fax/modem A peripheral that serves as both fax machine and modem. You can only send faxes that are files in the computer. Nearly all modems sold today include fax capability.

file All data stored on a computer is stored as files.

Firewire The catchy name for the IEEE 1394 standard. This is a high-speed computer port that supports data speeds up to 400 Mbps, and can be used for monitors, external hard drives, network connections, etc.

flash BIOS An upgradeable BIOS that allows the manufacturer to send you a floppy disk that will upgrade your BIOS to add features and capabilities that weren't available when your system was built. *See also* PnP.

flat-screen Refers to computer monitors. Early monitors had a screen that bulged out a lot in the middle, distorting text and making the monitors harder to read. A few years ago flat-screen monitors came on the market. Most are not truly flat, but are close enough that most users are quite comfortable with them. To add confusion, flat-panel displays, like those used in portable systems, are also becoming common. However, prices are still somewhat higher than for CRT monitors.

floppy drive A relic from 15 years ago, the 3.5" floppy is still used to back up small files or to transfer them from one computer to another. Although very little software now comes on 3.5" floppies, it is still too soon to go without one, as there are times when you just have to use one. Destined for the dust-bin of history, however, and none too soon.

FSB Front side bus. This is the connection between the CPU and the RAM. It is separated from the back side bus (*see* BSB) to speed up the systems as much as possible.

full tower A computer case that is 26–28" tall and is designed to sit on the floor beside or under your desk. It includes more drive bays for floppy drives, hard drives, etc., than regular cases, and usually has a bigger power supply.

G4 The latest version of the PowerPC CPU used in Macintosh systems.

GB Gigabyte, 1000 MB or a billion bytes. (*See* MB for more details and discussion.)

graphics adapter The part of the computer that controls what appears on the computer monitor. Also called a video card or a graphics controller.

handheld The category of computer smaller than a subnotebook. Their keyboards (if they have one at all) are generally too small for touch typing, and most now run Windows CE or the Palm OS.

hard drive The part of the computer that stores data and programs, even when the system is turned off.

heat sink A kind of radiator on top of a CPU that helps dissipate heat. The word sink in this case is used in its scientific sense, where "sink" is the opposite of "source," i.e., the CPU is a heat source, while the heat sink gets rid of it. Caution: A heat sink will do little good without an adequate flow of air across it.

hot swapping Changing out components without turning off the system. This is ONLY recommended in the case of PC Card peripherals running under Windows 98/ME/2000/XP, or for any USB component.

IDE Integrated Drive Electronics. The most common kind of hard drive and CD-ROM interface found in older PCs. *See* EIDE for more details.

inkjet A type of printer that makes its marks by squirting out tiny bursts of ink.

internal Refers to peripherals that are installed inside the computer case, but that can also be installed externally. Includes such things as fax/modems, CD-ROM drives, and even hard drives.

Internet A worldwide linkup of computers. These were mostly government and educational systems until the early 90s, when it was opened up to commercial and private users. Accessing the Internet is now one of the most popular uses for a computer. *See* Online Services.

I/O Input/output. Any sort of interface that transfers data in and out. Most commonly refers to a multi I/O card that provides two serial ports, a parallel port, and often controls the hard and floppy drives.

ISA Industry Standard Architecture. Also known as the AT bus. This is the computer slot that most cards and peripherals were designed to fit in until 1993. Most systems now come without any ISA slots. A motherboard can combine an ISA bus with PCI bus.

ISP Internet Service Provider. A company that provides a connection to the Internet via modem, but that doesn't provide much extra content. (*See also* Online Services.)

ISDN Integrated Services Digital Network is basically a digital telephone line. Most phone lines today still use analog technology, but many phone companies also make ISDN lines available. These can support data transfer rates up to 128 kbps rather than the 56 kbps available with standard modems on analog lines today. ISDN has now been overcome by other faster technologies without ever making much headway in the US. It is much more widely implemented in Europe and Japan.

Jaz A 1 or 2 GB removable drive from Iomega. Manufacture of these drives has been discontinued, but there are still many of them around.

joystick A type of controller used for many games.

jumpers A cheap and annoyingly common alternative to DIP switches. Many cards and motherboards have dual copper pins sticking up, often in rows, and to set various options, a jumper (a tiny flat black plastic rectangle) is placed over specific pairs of these pins to close a particular circuit. Should be history if PnP lives up to its promises, and not a day too soon.

K A thousand, or 1024, depending on the context. $1024=2^{10}$ or two to the tenth power. K is sometimes used in place of KB or kbps or other abbreviations that begin with K. The replacement is usually obvious from context.

KB Kilobyte. Again, it can be either 1000 bytes or 1024 bytes, depending on the context. *See* MB for further discussion.

kbps Kilobits per second. Usually refers to data transfer rate, and in this case, k equals 1000. Note also that the K is almost always uppercase, but because in this instance the letters following are lower case, the k also takes on the lower case.

kernel In Windows NT and its successors, the kernel is the core of the operating system The name derives from the fact that the kernel is the same regardless of which CPU the system will run on, with layers outside the kernel that account for all the various hardware differences of the various systems it may run on.

keyboard The most common way for people to communicate with a computer. The computer then communicates with the person via the monitor.

L2 cache Level 2 cache. This is the external SRAM cache. The internal cache built into 486 and higher CPUs is the L1 cache. Actually, the L2 cache is also built into all modern CPUs, but the name and distinction remain for design reasons.

laptops Portable computers that weigh 7–10 pounds, when weighed with their AC power supply, battery, and everything else needed to use them.

laser printer The most common printer used for business today. Provides several pages per minute of clear, easily readable output.

LCD Liquid crystal display. Used in everything from digital watches to flat panel displays, this is the easiest way to display electronic information with no moving parts.

lifetime toll-free tech support Means pretty much what it says. In theory it means for as long as you own the system, but it may wind up being the lifetime of the company that sold it to you.

lithium ion The latest in battery technology. Provides longer operation with less weight than NiCad or NMH.

local bus PCI or AGP slots on the motherboard that connect directly to the CPU and operate at 33, 66, or 133 MHz. Used for high-speed data transfer for video cards, network cards, and hard drive controllers.

log on To connect to an ISP or Online Service.

low radiation Monitors that give off very little electromagnetic radiation. They were developed a few years ago when concern about the possible health effects of electromagnetic radiation became widespread. The health effects are still uncertain, but virtually all new monitors are now low radiation. True flat-panel monitors, such as those used on portable systems, are zero-radiation.

Macintosh The primary alternative to the PC standard in the United States. Also known as Macs.

math coprocessor A chip or part of a CPU that is specifically designed to perform rapid math calculations. The 486DX, DX-2, DX4 and all Pentium class CPUs have math coprocessors built in, but 386s and 486SXs do not.

MB Megabyte. As with the difference in K, this can mean either 1,000,000 bytes or 1,048,576 bytes (2^{20}). Hard drive manufacturers like to use the 1,000,000 definition because it makes their drives look bigger. However FDISK, used to set up hard drives, uses the 1,048,576 value, so a hard drive that the manufacturer calls an 850 MB drive, for example, will show up on FDISK as 810 MB, causing users to wonder if they have been cheated or made a mistake. They have not. The number of bytes is the same either way.

Megapixel A million pixels. This refers to digital cameras that record over a million pixels of data when taking a picture. Typically a megapixel camera will have a resolution of 1280 × 960, or something close to that.

memory key Less common name for a **pen drive**.

MHz Megahertz, or million cycles per second. This is the way that the speed of CPUs is measured. The earliest PCs ran at 4.77 MHz, while Pentium IV CPUs can run internally at up to 3000 MHz (3 Gigahertz or GHz) or more. In this usage, Mega always means 1,000,000.

mid-tower A computer case, roughly 17" × 17" × 7", but designed to stand vertically. This has become the most popular case design in recent years.

mini-hub The central connector through which computers are networked together. The way network cables and network cards are designed, standard cables cannot simply connect two computers. Instead, each computer, up to as many as eight of them, are plugged into a mini-hub so they can communicate.

modem The device that allows computers to communicate over phone lines.

monitor The screen of a standard computer.

morphing Changing one image into another in a gradual process over several frames. Examples of this were first seen in the movies like "Willow" and "The Terminator," but are now being widely used, and are available in a number of home software packages so that home users can play with these techniques.

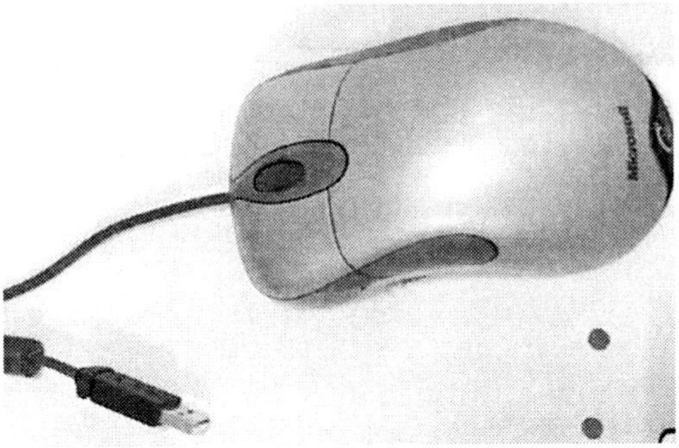

This is a USB mouse made by Microsoft.

motherboard The main system board inside the computer. This is where the CPU and RAM sit, and includes the slots where the various cards are installed.

mouse A pointing device that the user moves around by hand, moving a pointer on the monitor.

MPEG Motion Picture Experts Group. Refers to video that meets the standards developed by this group for displaying full-motion video on a computer screen. In reality, MPEG is a form of data compression.

ms Millisecond, or thousandth of a second. Used primarily to measure the speed of hard drives and CD-ROM drives.

MS-DOS Microsoft Disk Operating System. The primary operating system in use on PCs prior to Windows 95. The last version produced was 6.22, although the version embedded in Windows 95 is sometimes referred to as DOS 7.0.

multimedia A combination of moving pictures and sound on a computer. This is much more complex on a computer than it is on a TV, primarily because a computer uses digital rather than analog technology.

multisession Allows photographs and other data to be copied to a CD-ROM disk at different times (i.e., not all in one session), such that all photos/data can still be viewed at a later time.

Netscape A common Internet browser, although Microsoft's Internet Explorer now has more users.

network A means of connecting computers into a high-speed data transfer system so that they can communicate with each other at speeds close to those that are available from a hard drive. If you need more information on networks, there are whole books dedicated to them.

NiCad Nickel-Cadmium batteries. Originally, the most common type of battery used in portable systems. Rarely used these days, for a variety of reasons.

nickel metal hydride Now the low-end type of battery for use in portable systems. Provides a longer battery life than NiCad, and has better recharge characteristics, but is being overtaken by Lithium Ion technology, which is even better and lighter.

NiMH Abbreviation for Nickel Metal Hydride.

non-interlaced Refers to the preferred type of monitor. Often abbreviated as NI. Many early monitors, such as the IBM 8514A, would draw the odd lines on one pass, then come back and draw the even lines on the next pass. This is called interlacing. Non-interlaced monitors draw every line on every pass, and both the video card and the monitor should support a refresh rate of at least 70 Hz (i.e., it will redraw the screen at least 70 times per second) at the resolution you intend to use. Any lower number (usually 60 or less) will cause the monitor to flicker, which is annoying to say the least. All monitors sold today support NI use, but can still be set up to run in interlaced mode, which can be very wearing on the eyes.

notebooks Slang term for portable computers, although the term "notebook computer" is not slang.

ns Nanosecond or billionth of a second. Defines the speed of CPUs and RAM. A CPU running at 1 GHz completes each cycle in 1 ns.

OCR Optical Character Recognition. OCR software examines the patterns imported by a scanner or fax, and converts them to text. Accuracy depends on the scanner, the software, and the clarity of the original image.

OEM Original Equipment Manufacturer. Many companies do not provide their own warranty on parts, especially monitors and hard drives, but instead refer you back to the OEM for repairs and service. This can be very frustrating to users, when the tech support person at the company where they bought the computer says that they have to go to a third party for support on a given item.

online services Services that can be reached by computer and modem. They include AOL, Prodigy, and many others. Most now charge a flat-rate monthly fee for unlimited time on-line. The Internet is not technically an on-line service, but can be accessed through nearly all of them, as well as through **Internet service providers** that do nothing else. Typically, on-line services generate and maintain extensive resources for their users that are not generally available on the Internet, but in many cases users find that there is little added value in this material.

operating system For a computer to work, it must have a program that translates commands into a form that the computer can deal with. This is called the operating system, and is the first program that loads when the computer is turned on, or booted. If the computer fails to boot, then the operating system did not load, and nothing else will run. For years, MS-DOS was the standard operating system. Linux and Windows 2000/XP are 32-bit operating systems that have been available to PC users for several years, but until the advent of Windows XP, and now some of the latest releases of Linux, none of them were really suited to home use.

OS Abbreviation for operating system.

parallel Nearly every PC comes with a parallel port, which is used largely to connect a printer, although it is also used by many scanners and Zip Drives. *Note:* The cable that plugs into a parallel port is also referred to as a Centronics cable.

PC Personal Computer. (If your first guess was Politically Correct, then you are in the wrong book!) Today's PCs are generally used to run Windows programs. Although Macintoshes are sometimes categorized as PCs, the term usually refers to systems that can run some version of Windows.

PC Card Refers to credit-card-size cards that can be added to most portable systems to add memory, a modem, a network interface, or even a hard drive. Used to be called PCMCIA Cards.

PCI Peripheral Component Interconnect. The common upgrade slot found on all motherboards today, it is several times faster than the older ISA slot. All Pentium class systems support PCI.

PCMCIA *see* PC Card.

PDA Personal Digital Assistant. This can refer to any number of handheld computers, especially those without a keyboard. The Palm Pilot is probably the most popular of these.

pen drive Probably the slickest little file transfer device available today. Just 2–4 inches long, and small enough to fit in your pocket, but stick it in a USB port and you can carry away up to several hundred MB of data.

Pentium IV Intel's current CPU for desktop systems.

peripherals Items such as printers, scanners, modems, etc., that are not necessary for the operation of the computer itself, but that add functionality not present without them.

PIII Pentium III, although it can also be expressed as P3.

pixel Picture element. One dot on the screen of a monitor. Everything you see on a computer monitor (except fingerprints and dirt) is made up of combinations of pixels.

plotters Printers that produce oversized drawings, such as engineering or architectural drawings.

Plug and Play (PnP) Refers to PCs that self-configure, i.e., when a new card or peripheral is added, the computer can recognize and use it without the user having to make any changes, such as moving jumpers or setting dip switches. This requires both hardware and software to cooperate, which Windows 98/ME and Windows 2000 both do reasonably well, and Windows XP even better. The latest versions of Linux also handle PnP quite well. Unless the drivers are included in Windows, it also requires the user to insert a floppy disk or CD with the proper drivers for the new device.

port replicator Similar to a docking station, but with fewer options, and almost never the capability to support an external monitor. It allows a user to connect a laptop to several external devices and/or a network with a single connection.

ports The plugs in the back of a PC that allow various peripherals to be plugged in. *See also* Serial, Parallel, USB, network, video, and Firewire.

power supply The part of a computer that takes 115V AC and turns it into direct current at 3.3V, 5V, and 12V to run the various components of the computer.

Postscript A printer control language that controls very precisely how text and graphics print out.

print heads Both dot matrix and inkjet printers use print heads to control how ink is transferred to the paper.

printer The peripheral that takes what you see on the screen and puts it on paper.

RAM Random Access Memory. Also referred to as DRAM or Dynamic RAM. These are the SIMMs or DIMMs where the computer keeps the data it is working with as it runs. Memory disappears from RAM in a split second when power is turned off.

RDRAM Rambus DRAM is manufactured under a license from Rambus. It is faster than standard DRAM, but also costs around $1 per MB, versus less than $0.25 per MB for SDRAM. Manufacturers have developed **DDR** RAM as a means of speeding up SDRAM systems at a lower cost.

refresh A measure of how frequently a computer screen is redrawn. Typically, anything less than 70 Hz will cause many users to perceive an annoying flicker.

RISC Reduced Instruction Set Computing. RISC CPUs handle a smaller variety of operations, but handle them much faster, so that their overall speed is faster than CISC (C[omplex]ISC) CPUs like the Intel 80 × 86 line. The Pentium and Pentium Pro CISC CPUs now use a lot of RISC technology, while RISC CPUs now use a much larger instruction set, so the two technologies appear to be merging.

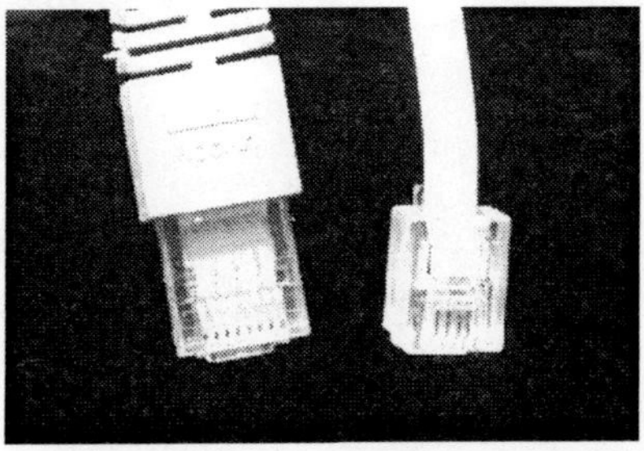

The RJ45 plug, on the left, is similar to, but a little larger than, the normal phone plug on the right.

RJ45 The plug that is most commonly used as a network connection. *See* picture.

scanner The opposite of a printer, in a way. The scanner takes paper documents and images and brings them into the computer.

SCSI Small Computer Systems Interface. A standard interface that can support up to seven peripherals, including hard drives, CD-ROM drives, scanners, etc.

SDRAM Synchronous DRAM. *See also* DIMM.

serial A type of port on the back of a computer. Most PCs have one or two serial ports, which is used for a mouse, an external modem, a PDA, or a variety of other peripherals. A serial port can have either 9 or 25 pins. Serial ports will disappear as USB peripherals become the standard.

server In a network, the computer that holds data or programs for a number of other computers (usually called clients), and that controls access to the network through logon names and passwords. A web server provides web pages on the internet.

SIMMs Single In-line Memory Modules. These were how RAM was installed in a computer before the advent of DIMMs.

single edge connector What the Pentium II/III fits into rather than a ZIF socket. Not compatible with original Pentium CPUs, and has become obsolete as the Pentium IV has moved back to a ZIF socket.

slot The electrical connection on a motherboard that allows cards to be added to the computer. *See also* bus.

software The programs that run on a computer.

SoundBlaster The leading brand of sound card, with which most other sound cards are at least nominally compatible.

spreadsheet One of the primary types of software. Used for accounting and numbers. Visicalc, one of the first spreadsheets, was a primary reason that the first Apple computers became popular, while Lotus 1-2-3 did the same for the IBM PC. Microsoft Excel is the leading spreadsheet today.

SSE Streaming SIMD Enhancements. SIMD is Single Instruction, Multiple Data, so SSE is an acronym within an acronym. Basically, it is supposed to be a way for the CPU to handle math coprocessor data more rapidly.

subnotebooks Portable computers that weigh less than four pounds, packed and ready to go. They usually do not have floppy drives or CD-ROM drives installed, although they may have external units that can be plugged in.

suite A combination of software packages, usually word processing, spreadsheet, presentation graphics, and database, all sold as a single package and designed to work closely together. Suites have been offered at very low prices compared to their individual components over the last several years, forcing software prices down in the office category.

SVGA Super VGA. Refers to resolutions above VGA or 640 × 480. The major SVGA resolutions are 800 × 600, 1024 × 768, 1280 × 1024, and 1600 × 1200.

tape backup A drive that allows you to back up the contents of a hard drive onto a magnetic tape for data protection and archiving.

thermal wax Refers to expensive, high quality color printers.

tower A computer case that is designed to stand on end. A full tower usually sits on the floor beside the desk, while a mini- or mid-tower is usually on the desk beside the monitor.

trackball A kind of upside down mouse with a big ball on top and buttons on each side.

Trackpoint™ This is IBM's trademarked name for a pointing device that looks like a pencil eraser and is embedded in the computer keyboard between the G, H, and B keys.

A Trackpoint button on a laptop keyboard.

trojan horse A program that appears to do one thing, while covertly doing something else, such as communicating with a remote computer and allowing a remote user to access or control the local machine. *See also* virus.

True-Type A scaleable font format developed by Microsoft and widely used in Windows.

UART Universal Asynchronous Receiver-Transmitter. Refers to a chip that stores (buffers) data during high-speed modem transfers so that it is less likely to be lost.

upgrade The process of paying a little more to get a better component when buying a computer. For example, you might upgrade from 128 to 256 MB RAM. Also, to add peripherals or increase capability of an older system by replacing or adding components.

upload *see* download.

UPS Uninterruptible Power Supply. A battery backup that provides power to a computer when the lights go out, or even flicker.

USB Universal Serial Bus. A new interface for PCs that will, in theory, support up to 126 devices (keyboard, mouse, modem, printer, scanner, joystick, video camera, etc.) on a single port. Perhaps one of the nicest things about USB is that it is hot swappable, meaning that you don't have to shut down and reboot just to add or remove a device. However, I don't know anyone who has gotten even close to 126 USB devices to work together at once. Most PCs come with two or four USB ports.

VGA Video Graphics Array. Refers to a color video display that is 640 pixels wide by 480 pixels high, and is the default resolution for Windows.

virus A program that copies itself onto any computer that it has access to, without the knowledge of the computer owner or user. While some viruses are relatively harmless, many are designed to corrupt the hard drive or data stored on it after a period of time. Anti-virus programs are designed to detect and destroy viruses.

voice mail This is the answering machine that gives you choices (Press 1 for Sales, Press 2 for ...), but that may completely block your access to a real human being.

voice recognition Voice recognition software allows you to talk into your computer through a microphone, and then converts your spoken words into text on your screen. Accuracy depends on how clearly you speak, the level of background noise, and on the quality of the microphone and sound card.

Windows The first widely used graphical user interface on PCs. It is now obsolete, although it is still in use on many systems.

Windows 2000 The successor to Windows NT, it incorporates all the stability and security of NT with PnP and many other nifty features, but is now being superceded by Windows XP.

Windows 98 Microsoft's update to Windows 95, and probably the most widely used operating system today. It has incorporated Internet Explorer as the browser for both hard drive and Internet, and has upgraded support for USB, FAT-32, and other improvements. It is disappearing in favor of Windows XP.

Windows ME The successor to Windows 98, it incorporates a lot of multimedia features, as well as many other new features, but is reputed to be less stable than Windows 98. Now that Windows XP Home is available, Windows ME will disappear even more quickly than Windows 98.

Windows NT A full 32-bit operating system that looks identical to the Windows 95 interface (ver. 4.0), but that is quite different underneath. It does not require DOS to run, and incorporates a number of security and networking features that are more advanced than earlier versions of Windows.

Windows XP The latest version of the Windows operating system, and comes in two versions, Home and Professional. Both versions are built on the same code base as Windows 2000. This means that it is far more stable and secure than any earlier home version of Windows, although the Professional version is only a minor upgrade to Windows 2000.

word processor Programs that allow the user to type in and manipulate words and text, sometimes in very elaborate ways. This is the most common use for PCs, except possibly for games and e-mail.

Xeon The server version of Intel's Pentium II/III CPU.

XGA Extended Graphics Array. Refers to a screen resolution of 1024 × 768 on a portable system.

ZIF Zero Insertion Force. Refers to a socket for the CPU that requires no force to remove the old one and insert a new one. Supposed to make upgrading your CPU easy and painless. Applies to Pentium IV systems, as well as the latest Duron and Athlon CPUs.

Zip Drive A drive from Iomega that uses a removable cartridge with a capacity of 100 MB, or 250 MB in the most recent version. A portable Zip drive connects to the parallel or USB port, making it very easy to use on several systems, while internal Zip drives use either an IDE or a SCSI connector. The Zip drive is the leading candidate to replace the 3.5" floppy drive.

INDEX